CAPITALISM
CREATED THE CLIMATE CRISIS

AND
CAPITALISM
WILL SOLVE IT

KENTARO KAWAMORI

CAPITALISM

CREATED THE CLIMATE CRISIS

AND

CAPITALISM

WILL SOLVE IT

THE MARKET FORCES CATALYZING
A CLIMATE TECHNOLOGY RENAISSANCE

WILEY

Published by John Wiley & Sons, Inc., Hoboken, New Jersey.
Published simultaneously in Canada.

For general information on our other products and services or for technical support, please contact our Customer Care Department within the United States at (800) 762-2974, outside the United States at (317) 572-3993 or fax (317) 572-4002.

Wiley also publishes its books in a variety of electronic formats. Some content that appears in print may not be available in electronic formats. For more information about Wiley products, visit our web site at www.wiley.com.

Library of Congress Cataloging-in-Publication Data is Available:

ISBN 9781394201556 (Cloth)
ISBN 9781394201563 (ePub)
ISBN 9781394201570 (ePDF)

Cover art: Maggie Duffy
Cover design: Maggie Duffy

SKY10075290_051624

To my family, friends, and all the entrepreneurs and those who support them building the future of climate solutions and a new energy economy.

Contents

Acknowledgments

THIS BOOK IS the culmination of my interactions with all the great people in my life who have helped me get to where I am today; there are so many of you. Thank you for being a part of my life and continuing to shape my journey.

Introduction

WE HAVE CREATED the perfect storm. Consumerism—the insatiable demand for more goods and services—powers our economic system of capitalism, which needs reliable, affordable, and easily available energy to produce the products that can be sold for profits. Most of our energy generation in its current forms creates excessive greenhouse gases (GHGs), including carbon dioxide and methane, that become trapped in our atmosphere and, like a blanket, warm our planet to excess.

The result is climate change, the long-term shifting of temperatures and weather patterns coupled with more extreme weather-related events and changes that threaten the livability of our planet.

Among all the negativity, though, there is positive news. Capitalism is purpose-built to provide the breeding ground for solutions to the climate crisis using the same creativity, tenacity, and drive that led to the crisis. Given the right set of incentives, we will turn capitalism into the driving force for the good of the planet.

Industrialization in the 17th century coincided with the beginning of the global temperature rise due to industry emissions and a growing population. Despite this long history between human activity and a warming planet, most of us still seem unwilling or unable to materially change our demands, perhaps from ignorance to the issue or lack of interest in getting involved. Even if we individually embrace sustainability, on an absolute basis, the global consumption of every resource will increase radically as planet Earth becomes home to nearly 10.5 billion people by 2100.[1] Future generations will face potential resource constraints and even depletion at our current trajectory.

For those individuals who still refute climate science, they will have trouble denying temperatures these days might seem a bit colder or hotter, and the weather is wetter or drier than they remember. They'll likely agree that the cost of goods and services has risen and on some days the air isn't quite as clean as it used to be.

Welcome to a world where our climate *is* changing and the world is reacting. Those reactions range from talk about climate shifts, carbon footprints, and severe weather events to companies raising prices to compensate for the cost of increased climate disruptions, global firms working to reduce GHG emissions, and groups in and outside of government brainstorming for solutions to the challenges.

While the climate crisis has recently seen a positive uptick in awareness, most historical climate talk did not result in immediate concerns for the general public. However, with regional climate activity becoming increasingly relevant in today's headlines, many need to rethink that "who-cares" attitude. In the last few years, Florida dealt with traumatic coastal flooding from severe hurricanes, Northern California coped with tremendous devastation from wildfires, and India sizzled under brutal heat. Earth's global surface temperatures have risen faster since 1970 than in any 50-year period over the past 2,000 years, according to the latest report from the nonprofit United Nation's Intergovernmental Panel on Climate Change.[2]

The days of ignoring climate change and its effects on our daily lives have come and gone. People across the world have awakened to the crisis and started to demand action; for example, a majority of adults in the United States want the country to prioritize developing renewable energy sources instead of expanding the production of fossil fuels like oil, coal, and natural gas, according to a recent poll from the Pew Research Center.

On the other side of the Atlantic, sentiments favoring our planet's sustainability run deep. The European Union (EU) in September 2023 revised upwards its renewable energy targets, with passage of a law requiring 42.5% of EU energy to be renewable by 2030.[3] That's almost double the 2022 level of 23%.[4]

European climate law also stipulates EU countries must cut GHG emissions by at least 55% by 2030. The goal is climate neutral—net zero GHG emissions—by 2050.[5]

And, let's not forget COP28, the UN Conference of Parties that met in late 2023 in Dubai to discuss what the world can do about the climate crisis. Accomplishments at the conference included a mid-term review (global stocktake) of progress countries are making toward commitments as part of the 2015 Paris Agreement and a decision to operationalize the Loss and Damage Fund adopted at COP27. The latter provides financial assistance to help developing countries cope with climate change issues.[6] Both developments are continued steps toward the nations of the world finding common ground on how best to combat climate shifts and their impacts on biodiversity and human life.

Capitalism Created the Climate Crisis and Capitalism Will Solve It isn't a book about pointing fingers or directing blame, bashing the oil and natural gas industry, or capitalism itself. Rather this book is about looking more closely at the past to better understand where we are today and gain insights into finding future solutions.

To state the obvious, no one wants an unlivable planet. But so much of the talk and writing about climate is tainted with misinformation, disinformation, whitewashing, greenwashing (the environmental version of whitewashing), and outright lies. Sorting through all that makes it even more difficult for corporations and individuals to know what's the truth.

In these pages, readers will gain a clear picture of how and why capitalism created the climate crisis, why it perpetuates, and how with the right mindset and direction—a marriage of public and private interests—and the help of capitalism we can better understand the vast opportunities that lie ahead of us.

The book is divided into two parts. The first looks at the state of our climate, why we should be concerned, and how we got to where we are. That includes a discussion of fossil fuels—good and not so good, how capitalism and governance helped perpetuate disposable commerce, and how climate risk equates to financial risk in this new era of accountability. In Part II, I'll cover why capitalism is the key to solving the crisis, explore how modern finance is powering the next wave of innovative solutions that enable the world to decarbonize, examine the energy transition revolution, and finally share why I am hopeful for our future climate state of affairs.

As a consultant to numerous energy firms and a former C-suite executive at a Fortune 500 oil and gas firm, Chesapeake Energy Corporation, I've witnessed firsthand the challenges and opportunities within the traditional energy sector. As an entrepreneur and CEO of Persefoni AI Inc., I now lead the way in developing critical solutions in support of democratizing carbon accounting. My combined experiences in energy markets and climate technology give me a nuanced understanding of how market forces can be harnessed to spur climate action. Capitalism's inherent drive for innovation and efficiency can be an invaluable tool in developing and scaling up climate technologies.

While working at energy firms in the oil and gas and utilities sectors, the picture of capitalism on a collision course with sustainability became clear. I saw firsthand how the conversation in the industry began changing. Fueled by everything from social protests led by Greta Thunberg and environmental activists in boardrooms, the industry began the transition to new forms of energy and readily acknowledged its role in the climate fight.

I recognized we couldn't solve the problem without better understanding the problem itself. That meant we needed a better way to measure carbon emissions against a common climate baseline. Today, that's known as carbon accounting, or sustainable finance. Measurement, though, is just the beginning of the journey to decarbonization.

In 2019, I left Chesapeake, and the next year Persefoni was born. We named the company after the Greek goddess Persephone. Her story is one of sadness and redemption. Among other things, she is the goddess of spring. It is the themes of rebirth and bloom associated with spring that we wanted reflected in the company's name, an inherent optimism that things will get better.

Whatever your background or expertise or your level of climate knowledge, *Capitalism Created the Climate Crisis and Capitalism Will Solve It* will clearly lay out the issues and problems, along with a path to solid solutions. Whether someone believes or not in the possibility of a silver bullet to reverse the effects of a warming planet overnight, it's highly unlikely any solution will happen without what's discussed in this book. Together we can make a difference for our planet.

A final note: a degree of fear, stress, and pessimism creeps into nearly every discussion on climate. In these pages, I choose to be hopeful. The book's tone doesn't belabor the negative; rather, it focuses on a future in which we successfully rise to the challenge and first mitigate, then reverse, the damage to our planet.

I believe capitalism can be a powerful engine for climate action, but only if we design the right incentives and frameworks. Are you ready to explore how we can achieve this together?

PART

I

Where We Are Today

1

Collision Course

Consumerism, Capitalism, and Climate Crisis

"By all empirical measures, no economic system other than capitalism has created greater prosperity for citizens or contributed to more breakthrough technology and economic advancements in the history of human civilization."

I WAS ON stage at TechCrunch's "TC Sessions: Climate 2022." It was mid-June and I was surrounded by an overwhelmingly left-leaning crowd on the University of California–Berkeley campus when I began to share my mantra:

Capitalism created the climate crisis and capitalism will solve it.

I had expected at least some fallout from this progressive crowd, but instead, there was only silence, so I continued.

Global consumerism—the world's endless demand for goods and services—powers our capitalism. Governments, in turn, provide rules and regulations that support this economic system of private ownership for profit. Capitalism needs access to cheap, reliable energy to produce products and eventually profits. Generating that energy—primarily through burning of fossil fuels—generates green-house gases (GHGs) that act like a blanket in our atmosphere, hold in more heat from the sun, and warm our planet to excess.

The bottom line: we as consumers have brought together the perfect set of ingredients that today manifest as Earth's climate crisis. This long-term alteration of temperature and weather patterns is fueled by trapped GHGs including carbon dioxide and methane (also sometimes known under the broad umbrella *carbon* or CO_2). The results are more frequent and severe heat waves, droughts, natural disasters, hurricanes, wildfires, and rising sea levels that can lead to flooding and the loss of coastal habitats. Rapidly melting polar ice caps also shrink animal habitats.

The long-term effects of these climate shifts are devastating, and not just on weather, sea levels, and animals. Estimates are that unaddressed climate change could cut global economic output by $23 trillion by 2050, according to Swiss Re, a leading global insurer based in Zurich, Switzerland.[1]

Consider these climate statistics:

- Earth is 1.1 degrees Celsius (°C) warmer today than in the late 1800s. A rise of 1.5°C above preindustrial levels is considered the maximum upper limit to avoid the worst fallout from climate change.[2]
- 2023 was Earth's hottest year on record.[3] Previously 2020 and 2016 statistically tied as the hottest, continuing a long-term warming trend.[4]
- June, July, and August 2023 was the hottest summer since 1880 when global record-keeping began.[5]
- Earth's atmosphere contains more carbon dioxide today than at any time in human history; 422.33 parts per million (ppm) as of December 30, 2023.[6] That compares with 290 ppm from 1800 to 1870.[7]
- Summer Arctic sea ice extent is shrinking by 12.2% per decade due to warmer temperatures, affecting ocean circulation and water temperatures.[8]

The Power of Capitalism

As the numbers reflect, our climate is in trouble, with consumerism and its need for energy to produce goods the leading culprits. But before anyone—no matter their politics—assumes all it takes to save our planet is an anti-capitalistic agenda, consider that capitalism also is purpose-built to provide the breeding ground for solutions to our climate challenges.

We as consumers and the governments that we elect can take control of and learn to alleviate the climate problem with the same creativity, tenacity, and drive that led to the crisis.

Capitalism at Work

Tesla, a publicly traded company, and SpaceX, a private company as of this writing, are examples of companies at the forefront of leading the change in their respective industries. Tesla, cofounded by Elon Musk, almost singularly reshaped the automotive landscape with its first commercial EV, and so much so that by 2022 nearly all major automobile manufacturers have competitive EV lines. The popularity of Tesla sparked the competition needed among manufacturers to propel EVs into the mainstream of the auto industry, while bringing innovations like self-driving mode and remote software updates for onboard computer systems.

Tesla is capitalism at work, where a company sees an opportunity and builds toward it. The market rewards the company for its innovation while competitors seeking similar rewards flock to the new idea. Through competition, a market that was previously written off has become not just mainstream, but the future of the auto industry.

Similarly SpaceX helped reshape and resurge space exploration from what was primarily run by government agencies—NASA in the United States, for example—into now private companies. Founded in 2002 also by Musk, SpaceX has changed the way people think about the potential for space travel and the possibility of the colonization of other planets.

The ideas of space travel and the concept of colonizing other planets aren't new. What is new, though, is that SpaceX is advancing how these ideas can be achieved and with reusable space delivery vehicles. The company's work ultimately will drop the unit economics to a point where more innovation from the private sector propels the idea of space travel into mainstream reality for many.

Life-Changing Outcomes

I am pro-capitalism; I'm also an entrepreneur. I see the world through both lenses and I firmly believe that through the combination of capitalism, entrepreneurship, and, where warranted, government intervention, many of the most challenging problems we face today—including climate change—can be solved.

Capitalism's contributions toward quality of life, economic growth, and incomes worldwide have been profound. No economic system has created greater prosperity for citizens or contributed to more break-through technology and economic advancements in the history of human civilization.

Though exact numbers vary among data sources, the positive effects of capitalism on poverty levels are indisputable. In the early 1800s, 75% to 80% of the world's population experienced extreme poverty. By 2018, that number had fallen to about 10%.[9] In other words, capitalism brought vast swaths of human civilization out of poverty. It will bring human civilization out of climate despair. The move is already under way.

Finally, my skeptical audience in that California auditorium began to understand the complexities of the relationship between capitalism and climate change, that capitalism isn't all bad, and in fact can give hope to our climate's future.

The World Begins to React

The world—from boardrooms to governments and individuals—is reacting to what's happening with our climate. Those reactions range from climate-related headlines that dominate the news to more frequent severe weather events, the latest on greenhouse gas emissions, word of companies raising prices to compensate for the cost of increased climate regulation, and the latest on investors demanding globally responsible firms that work to reduce carbon emissions. Governments are spearheading landmark environmental legislation, too.

Until relatively recently, unless someone was a staunch environmentalist, a lot of the talk about climate change seemed a bit distant to really care. After all, if someone lives in Florida, why should it matter if the Arctic ice sheet melts? Or, if an Ohio manufacturing company relies on raw materials from wildfire-prone areas like California or Canada, or if a technology employer relies on remote talent from India?

Today those climate-fueled changes make a big difference not only in quality of life but also to our capitalistic, profit-based economy's all-important bottom lines. In 2022 and 2023, Florida was pummeled with traumatic coastal flooding and multiple catastrophic hurricanes that wiped away cities and threatened to bankrupt insurance companies.[10] Since 2017, 11 companies that used to offer homeowners insurance in the state have liquidated.[11] Californians battled colossal wildfires that devastated towns and economies. Some insurance companies have stopped writing policies or reduced their offerings in California[12] as climate risks outweigh profits. Meanwhile, India and its people have suffered through increasingly brutal, deadly heat.

In 2023, Canada also saw wildfires that burned a record 45.7 million acres.[13] In addition to destruction caused directly by those fires, huge swaths of North America were blanketed with heavy and choking particulate air pollution that blocked out the sun and affected tens of millions of people.

A few decades ago, events like these stacking up in rapid succession were rare. Not so anymore. The days of ignoring the climate crisis and its effects on our daily lives have expired. "The era of global warming has ended; the era of global boiling has arrived," UN Secretary General Antonio Guterres said in July 2023.[14]

Even those who shade climate science have trouble denying that no matter where they are in the world, temperatures these days seem a bit colder or warmer, and that the days are wetter or drier than they remember. They'll likely agree that the cost of goods and services has gone up.

The climate crisis *is* true, it's real, and capitalism will solve it. As more people and companies recognize our climate emergency, sustainability has gained traction in boardrooms and on Wall Street. Consumers now demand environmental, social, and governance (ESG), also known as socially responsible, investing for their own portfolios as well as from the companies they invest in. Estimates suggest that ESG-aligned assets under management are projected to reach $10.5 trillion by 2026, representing 20% of the total market. That's a significant increase from $4.5 trillion in 2021.

ESG: What Does It Mean?

ESG is an acronym for environmental, social, and governance. In investment terms, ESG is also known as sustainable investing, socially responsible investing, and impact investing.

- **Environmental.** *Could relate to a company's impact on the environment or the risks and opportunities associated with the impacts of climate change on the company, its business, and its industry.*
- **Social.** *Can focus on the company's relationship with people and society, or whether the company invests in its community.*
- **Governance.** *Can relate to company operations and executive compensation.*

Source: Investor.gov.[15]

A Look Back to Move Forward

Climate change is not a new phenomenon; greenhouse gasses have been building in Earth's atmosphere since the Industrial Revolution began in the 18th century.[16] Scientists have been predicting or measuring the changes for hundreds of years.[17]

In 1824, French mathematician and physicist Joseph Fourier determined something in our atmosphere was acting like a blanket to keep Earth warmer than it should be.[18] A little more than two decades later, in 1856, amateur scientist Eunice Foote discovered that blanket was made up of carbon dioxide and water vapor, and that this trapped escaping infrared radiation (heat) in our atmosphere, warmed the planet.[19]

It wasn't until 1938 that another amateur scientist, Guy Callendar, first recorded actual estimates of global warming. A steam engineer by trade, he discovered temperatures globally had climbed 0.3°C in the previous 50 years. Callendar blamed industry carbon dioxide emissions for the rise, but scientists basically ignored him.[20]

While the links between human activity and climate change haven't materialized in systematic change, history warrants a closer look in our quest to embrace sustainability.

Modern Capitalism

To more clearly understand how we contribute to our changing climate, let's look at capitalism itself and the market incentives created by it.

Capitalism as an economic system has evolved significantly over time thanks mostly to innovations in technology and financing. Although capitalism's exact origins are the subject of debate, the roots of modern capitalism can be traced back to the 16th and 17th centuries in Europe when merchants began to develop more sophisticated systems of trade and finance and accumulated wealth through trade and investment. As the ideas of private property and the pursuit of profit became more prominent, feudalism transitioned to capitalism, a system in which production, distribution, and exchange are based on market forces rather than feudal relationships or state control.

Over time, capitalism has undergone many changes, spread to other parts of the world, and taken on multiple forms. In terms of its forms, for example, communist China's capitalism differs from its more democratic form in the United States because of the dominance of the Communist Chinese Party and state-owned enterprises, though it does allow for some private profits.

Today, capitalism is the dominant economic system in the world. This evolution to modern capitalism led to a symbiotic relationship with the fossil-fuel industry as the need for dependable, cheap energy also mushroomed.

Tenets of Modern Capitalism

- *Private property, including the means of production like factories, land, and other resources, is owned and controlled by private individuals or corporations, rather than by the state or feudal lords.*
- *A market-based economy based on the production, distribution, and exchange of goods and services is primarily determined by the supply and demand of the market.*
- *The pursuit of profits through growth and expansion with economic self-interests is maximized through consumerism.*
- *There is innovation and creativity not only in product and delivery but also in finance.*

Source: Our World in Data.[21]

The Rise of Climate Science

In the grand scheme of all human knowledge, climate science is a very new discipline. Although scientists first identified the greenhouse effect in the 1800s, they didn't begin to study the impact of human activities, such as burning fossil fuels and deforestation, on the Earth's climate until the 1900s. It wasn't until the 1980s that the term *climate change* became more widely used as research showed that human activities were contributing to rising temperatures and other changes in the Earth's climate.

The bottom line is the biggest long-term risk to our global economy is climate change. Without mitigating action taken now, the world's total economic value will shrink and the physical risks resulting from climatic events will rise to over $100 billion per year in the United States. By the end of this century, the increase in global temperatures could cause damages equal to 7% to 11% of annual global GDP per year according to a study reference by the White House.[22]

Elements in Place for Solutions

It's taken people, companies, and economies plenty of time to digest the negative effects of rampant alterations in climate. But as more governments and consumers see the environmental threat to their ways of life, they also are waking up to the potential for solutions.

Capitalism, with its strong motive for profit, innovation, and technological progress, will be the force to change things yet again, and spearhead climate correction in the process. After all, economic history shows that most innovations come in response to events, specific problems, and new technological opportunities.[23]

■ ■ ■

As consumers react to what's happening to our climate, and demand more sustainability, capitalism-led innovation will be the driving force behind change. Governments will establish rules and regulations that reflect the demands of their constituents, and companies will rally their innovation teams to find sustainable solutions that deliver.

For example, where once unapproachable costs made alternatives to greenhouse-gas-producing fossil fuels less attractive and more expensive, that's changed as consumer sentiments favor sustainability. Two-thirds of adults in the United States want the country to prioritize developing renewable energy sources instead of expanding the production of fossil fuels like oil, coal, and natural gas, according to a recent poll from the Pew Research Center. The same study found that almost half (48%) of all Americans ages 18 to 29 want the United States to phase out greenhouse-gas-producing fossil fuels and "exclusively use renewables."[24]

Rise of Alternative Energy Sources

With the introduction of consumer-driven sentiments that favor net zero (zero greenhouse gas emissions) as well as financial incentives, governments, countries, and companies are exploring and building out alternative energy sources to meet consumer demands. Some are more feasible today than others.

I'll look in-depth at alternative energy sources to fossil fuels later. In the meantime, though, here are a few synergistic solutions already producing results:

- **Electric vehicles (EVs).** Globally in 2022, electric vehicles made up 10% of all passenger vehicle sales, 10 times the number sold a decade ago. EVs made up 6% of sales in the United States that year, but a whopping 80% of those in Norway, and 22% in China.[25]

- **Wind and other renewable energies.** In the European Union, renewable energy accounted for only 12.5% of energy needs in 2010. By 2021, those numbers climbed to 21.8% thanks to incentives from the EU's Renewable Energy Directives.[26] The 2022 invasion of Ukraine by Russia, a main EU oil and natural gas provider, further accelerated the EU move away from fossil fuels.
- **Solar energy.** The use of solar energy is growing so fast it could completely displace fossil fuels from the global economy before 2050, according to the World Economic Forum. In 2022 solar capacity exceeded 1 terawatt (1,000 gigawatts) and is still growing by 20% a year. If that capacity growth persists, by 2031, solar could top the combined total of coal, gas, nuclear, and hydro in terms of the source of energy production.[27]

As market trends indicate growth in alternative energy sources and solutions, investments will soon quickly follow from the growing interest of consumers and businesses.

The Power of Finance

A great analogy of the role of financial markets on capitalism, and its effect on climate change, is that capitalism is the base element of a fire, modern finance the jet fuel poured over it, and the result a conflagration.

Whereas the concept of lending money is as old as humanity itself, the birth of organized financial markets gave way to financial innovations that would provide the necessary capital for ventures large and small to expand around the globe. That growth, though, came with the corresponding rise in global emissions.

Our Modern System

Delving deeper into how capitalism works, today's financial system relies on financial instruments and institutions like banks and stock exchanges to facilitate the exchange of money, goods, and services.

These markets also played a crucial role in the Industrial Revolution by issuing stocks and bonds for purchase by investors that provided the necessary capital for industrialization.

Financial markets then, and now, also facilitated the movement of capital from one critical new industrial sector to another, as people sought the most promising opportunities for investment to generate profits. Along the way, these markets also created new financial instruments like insurance and futures contracts to help mitigate risk and increase the efficiency of transactions.

Then Came Wall Street

Like so many things in recent centuries, Americans take nascent concepts and scale them to previously unimaginable heights. Think New York City as the world's financial center, and Wall Street as an industry, the star player.

Although New York City has been a financial center for much of its history, it really began to emerge as a global financial hub in the late 19th and early 20th centuries. During this time, New York City attracted many financial institutions and became a center for international trade and finance. The New York Stock Exchange, founded in 1792,[28] set the rules for trading stocks and bonds on Wall Street, and quickly became the largest and most important stock exchange in the United States, playing a central role in the development of the US financial system.

More new financial instruments were developed and built out on Wall Street, including derivatives, futures, and mutual funds.

These details are important in the development of the climate crisis because these financial instruments encouraged investments and development that required quick, cheap, and dependable energy to produce more goods and services. Burning coal, oil, and natural gas to create that energy led to the accelerated release of greenhouse gases into the atmosphere.

Ruthless Capitalism

Wall Street's innovations also helped introduce a ruthlessly American form of capitalism not seen before with an extreme focus on financial performance and profits. By the 20th century, Wall Street became the birthplace of market-moving financial analysis and research. New forms of information technology fueled the advanced analysis and research being adopted by the industry. New investor classes like corporate raiders and activist investors and the private equity industry were born.

All of this contributed to the export of economic and financial knowledge to new markets around the world—a key driver in the world economy's globalization. These new investors saw profit as something that could be engineered from existing companies' balance sheets and operations, and they prized cash flows above all else. That affected not only the companies targeted for takeover but also created a new dimension of thinking in boardrooms across the world as the realities of hostile investors taking over a company quickly became commonplace. This led to a new perspective on profits, intensifying fear of financial underperformance and incentivizing practices that would harm our climate at unprecedented levels. (See "Earth by the Numbers" for details.)

Earth by the Numbers: Emissions and Population

1900:
- *Population: 1.65 billion*
- *Total CO_2 emissions: 1.95 gigatons*
- *CO_2 emissions per human: 1.18 metric tons*

1930:
- *Population: 2 billion*
- *Total CO_2 emissions: 3.94 gigatons*
- *CO_2 emissions per human: 1.97 metric tons*

1960:
- *Population: 3 billion*
- *Total CO_2 emissions: 9.39 gigatons*
- *CO_2 emissions per human: 3.13 metric tons*

1980:

- *Population: 3.7 billion*
- *Total CO_2 emissions: 19.48 gigatons*
- *CO_2 emissions per human: 5.26 metric tons*

2000:

- *Population: 6.15 billion*
- *Total CO_2 emissions: 25.5 gigatons*
- *CO_2 emissions per human: 4.15 metric tons*

2010:

- *Population: 7 billion*
- *Total CO_2 emissions: 33.31 gigatons*
- *CO_2 emissions per human: 4.76 metric tons*

2022:

- *Population: 7.98 billion*
- *Total CO_2 emissions: 37.15 gigatons*
- *CO_2 emissions per human: 4.66 metric tons*

Source: Worldometer, Statista.[29]

Applying the Brakes

Humankind globally has emitted more carbon dioxide into Earth's atmosphere since 1990 than in all of human history before that time. From the dawn of the Industrial Revolution to 1990, the world produced 807 billion tons of CO_2. Since 1990, we've produced 961 billion more tons.[30]

As corporations, individuals, organizations, and governments recognize the negative impact of greenhouse gas emissions, capitalism and minds are evolving. People have begun to rethink the US approach to capitalism that puts profits before all else.

Financial leaders on Wall Street have begun to refocus and look at investing in green technology. Sustainability has moved from the anti-capitalism category to a pro-capitalism driving force. Even the fossil fuel industry has picked up on the value of sustainability and its potential for profits. Many of the oil and gas majors are involved in research and development of alternate sources of energy.

A few more examples of the shifting consumer sentiment as reflected in dollars and cents include the following facts:

- In 2015, Norway banned its state pension fund, the world's largest sovereign wealth fund, from investing in coal companies.[31]
- In 2021, ABP, the Dutch pension fund for civil servants and teachers, said it would no longer invest in producers of oil, gas, and coal, and that it would dispense with its current investments in those sectors in 2023.[32]
- The $240 billion Australia Retirement Trust also has ramped up pressure on companies to hit net zero. In September 2023, the pension giant committed to cut carbon emissions by 43% by 2030 on its path to net zero by 2050.[33]
- In 2016, Johnson & Johnson, the New Jersey–based global health products conglomerate, signed a 12-year deal to buy 100 megawatts of wind power production from a wind farm in Colbecks Corner, Texas, near Amarillo. The purpose was to provide the equivalent of more than 60% of J&J's electricity use in the United States and 25% of its global use. J&J has set the goal of carbon neutrality by 2030.[34]

Sustainability has become a mainstream investment consideration. Money managers are stewards of other people's hard-earned money and have a fiduciary duty to act in the best interest of the beneficiary and consider all potential risks to maximize returns.

How can you be a good steward of someone else's money if asset managers are investing in corporations that are making the world that you live in worse off? The answer is, you can't. Investment decisions can significantly affect the well-being of the future generations. I'll talk more about the role of modern finance, Wall Street, and private equity in solving the climate crisis in Chapter 7.

The Big Picture: A Chapter Roundup

- Our global consumerism powers capitalism through cheap, readily available, reliable energy to produce products and eventually profits. That energy comes from burning fossil fuels which release greenhouse gases that warm our planet to excess. This super heating has led to climate change.
- The year 2023 was Earth's hottest on record. Previously 2020 and 2016 statistically tied as the hottest, continuing the long-term warming trend.[35]
- Unaddressed, climate shifts could cut global economic output by $23 trillion by 2050.[36]
- Capitalism with its inherent creativity, innovation, and tenacity, is purpose-built to provide the breeding ground for solutions to the climate crisis.
- Humankind globally has emitted more carbon dioxide into Earth's atmosphere since 1990 than in all of human history before that time.[37]
- Sustainability has moved from the anti-capitalism category to a pro-capitalism driving force. Even the fossil fuel industry has picked up on the profit potential of sustainability; many major players are involved in research and development of alternate forms of energy.

2

A Primer on Climate
Change Today

"Like a fire, capitalism will illuminate or burn. Its moral value hinges not on its core but on the hands that wield it."

OUR CLIMATE IS in trouble. Earth experienced its hottest 12-month period in recorded history from November 2022 to October 2023.[1] Even more concerning, as I write this book, Earth has just experienced the warmest month on record—July 2023—with a global mean air temperature of 16.95°C (62.51°F).[2]

To better understand the nuances of climate change today and into the future, and to help make your own informed decisions from a position of knowledge, let's start with a few more climate basics. If you're already an expert, consider this a quick refresher on some of the details.

What Is Climate Change?

As defined previously, climate change is the long-term shift in weather patterns and temperatures. Though some global warming and climate change can occur naturally, since the Industrial Revolution, Earth's warming has been driven primarily by human activities.

Specifically, the burning of fossil fuels to create energy generates the majority of greenhouse gases (GHGs). Those gases, including methane and CO_2, end up trapped in our atmosphere, act like a blanket, and warm the planet to excess. GHGs drive changes in our climate, bringing extreme heat, droughts, sea-level rise, and unpredictable weather events with potentially disastrous effects for humanity.

Global Warming Versus Climate Change

- **Global warming.** *Rise in global temperatures due mainly to the increasing concentrations of GHGs in the atmosphere.*
- **Climate change.** *Increasing changes in weather patterns, precipitation, temperatures, and wind patterns over a long period.*

Source: US Geological Survey.[3]

GHGs Defined

GHGs are gases trapped in our atmosphere that absorb infrared radiation (heat) emitted from Earth and warm the planet. The resulting climbing temperatures lead to change in precipitation patterns, storm severity, and rising sea levels, according to the US Energy Information Agency.

The vast majority of GHG is carbon dioxide (CO_2); the term sometimes also is used as a catch-all moniker for GHGs. Other GHGs include the following:

- Methane (CH_4)
- Nitrous oxide (N_2O)
- Chlorofluorocarbons (CFCs)
- Hydrofluorocarbons (HFCs)
- Perfluorocarbons (PFCs)
- Sulfur hexafluoride (SF_6)
- Nitrogen trifluoride (NF_3)

- *Sulfur oxides (SOx, SO$_2$)*
- *Nitrogen oxides (NOx, NO$_2$)*

Source: US Energy Information Agency.[4]

Fossil fuels like coal, natural gas, and petroleum are hydrocarbons, meaning they are made up of primarily carbon and hydrogen. When they are combusted or burned, the oxygen combines with carbon to form CO_2 and with hydrogen to form water H_2O. The chemical reaction releases heat, which is what we use today as a form of usable energy. The amount of CO_2 emissions depends on the carbon content of the fuel. Take coal for example: it has a higher carbon content, which will produce more CO_2 per unit of energy compared to fuels with lower carbon content like methane, also known as natural gas. For this reason, natural gas is often represented as the transitional step away from coal power generation as it can lead to immediate reductions of emissions.

Zeroing in on the numbers, fossil fuel combustion led to about 73% of total human-caused (anthropogenic) GHG emissions in the United States in 2021 (see Figure 2.1). Even though not all fossil fuels produce the same amount of GHGs, the combustion of petroleum products produced the most emissions (see Figure 2.2).

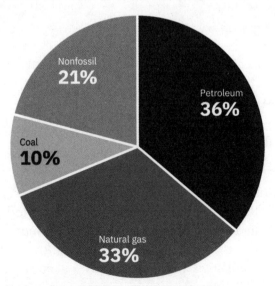

Figure 2.1   Energy consumption

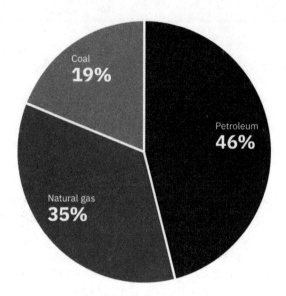

Figure 2.2   Energy-related CO$_2$ emissions

Here's a comparison of US energy consumption by source and the related CO$_2$ emissions by source for 2022, according to the US Energy Information Administration:

Energy Consumption

- Petroleum: 36%
- Natural gas: 33%
- Coal: 10%
- Nonfossil: 21%

Energy-Related GHG Emissions

- Petroleum: 46%
- Natural gas: 35%
- Coal: 19%[5]

From a global perspective, China is the biggest emitter of GHGs with 31% of global CO$_2$ emissions in 2021. That's followed by the United States at 14% of emissions; the EU, 8%; India, 7%; Russia, 5%; and Japan, 3%, according to numbers from the Global Carbon Project.[6] Before judging China too harshly, remember China also is one of the world's biggest manufacturers especially for developed countries. "Made in China" is big business across the globe.

Climate Terminology

- **Carbon accounting.** The process of quantifying and tracking the GHG emissions produced by private and public organizations.
- **Carbon footprint.** An estimate of how much carbon dioxide and other GHGs is produced to support your lifestyle or organization; usually measured in units of carbon dioxide equivalent (CO_2e).
- **Carbon neutral.** Focuses on balancing an entity's carbon emissions with carbon removals, typically achieved through sustainable carbon offset programs.
- **Decarbonization.** The process of reducing or eliminating carbon emissions.
- **ESG.** An acronym for environmental, social, and governance; the three pillars by which an organization's sustainability can be measured.
- **Greenhouse gases (GHGs).** Often referred to in general as carbon dioxide/CO_2, though also applies to additional types of gases.
- **Greenhouse Gas Protocol (GHGP).** Created in 1997, the GHGP is the original carbon accounting standard that provides guidelines for organizations to develop GHG emissions inventories.
- **Greenwashing.** The act of portraying a more sustainable, ethical, or "green" image of a company for marketing purposes.
- **ISSB.** The International Sustainability Standards Board established by the International Financial Reporting Standards Foundation (IFRS) to create high-quality sustainable standards that address investors' informational needs.
- **Net zero.** Refers to negating the amount of carbon (used as a general term for GHGs) a company emits by withdrawing the same amount through offsets and having it stored permanently in carbon sinks (carbon sequestration); common target for organizations to commit to is by 2050.
- **(The) Paris Agreement.** A legally binding international treaty that aims to limit global warming to below 1.5°C, compared with preindustrial levels.

(continued)

(continued)
- **Science-based target (SBTs).** *Emission-reduction goals that align with the necessary level of decarbonization to keep the global temperature increase below 2°C above preindustrial levels, as outlined in the Paris Agreement.*
- **Sustainable finance.** *Financial practices and investments that prioritize ESG factors, aiming to generate both financial returns and positive, sustainable outcomes for the planet and society.[7]*

A Look Back at Climate Change

In addition to the discovery, identification, and measurement of GHGs that warm our planet, globally there also have been crucial climate discoveries, revelations, and declarations through key global attempts to work toward solutions to the climate crisis.

To clarify, net-zero emissions or net zero refers to the neutralization of all GHGs, and carbon neutral refers only to the neutralization of carbon dioxide (CO_2) in the atmosphere.[8] Sometimes, mistakenly they're used interchangeably.

Let's briefly look at some of the milestones related to our changing climate.

Measure of CO_2 Levels

In 1958, geochemist Charles David Keeling was the first to measure the carbon dioxide level in our atmosphere accurately and demonstrate that it was rising. More important, Keeling analyzed his CO_2 samples and determined the rise was due to the use of fossil fuels.

Until Keeling took his measurements from atop Mauna Loa volcano in Hawaii and studied the results, scientists had only been able to generally hypothesize that fossil fuels were to blame for the higher levels of CO_2. Worth noting is that daily CO_2 concentrations taken at Mauna Loa continue today and are now known as the Keeling Curve, the longest continuous record of CO_2 concentrations in the world.[9]

Earth's Climate Model

In 1967, researchers produced the first accurate computer model of Earth's climate. That model by Syukuro Manabe and Richard Wetherald predicted that doubling concentrations of CO_2 could raise global temperatures by 2°C.

The model also enabled researchers to understand the impacts of different levels of CO_2 on global temperatures. Since the 1880s, CO_2 levels have gone up about 50% and temperatures increased by 1.1°C.[10]

Clean Air and Clean Water Acts

The Clean Air Act of 1970 defines the US EPA (Environmental Protection Agency) responsibilities for protecting and improving the nation's air quality and the stratospheric ozone layer. The last major change in the law, the Clean Air Act Amendments of 1990, was enacted by Congress in 1990. Legislation passed since then has made several minor changes.[11]

The Clean Water Act, first enacted in 1948 as the Federal Water Pollution Control Act, was reorganized and expanded in 1972 as the Clean Water Act. It lays out the basic structure for regulating discharges of pollutants into the waters of the United States and regulating quality standards for surface waters.[12]

Both of these laws have been instrumental in improving air and water quality in the United States. And that's not marketing speak. Once polluted rivers in the United States now flow cleaner, and the same with industrial plants that once constantly belched choking pollution into the air. The EPA has played a critical role in researching and understanding climate change through scientific programs and data collection. They've also worked with companies to help them better understand their datasets.

The EPA, though, has faced criticism for not taking harsher actions to curb GHG emissions. It's worth keeping in mind that like any large government agency, actions take time. Plus, the EPA is subject to political pressure and interference, which hampers progress.

IPCC Begins

More globally in 1988, the United Nations Environment Programme and the World Meteorological Organization (WMO) established the Intergovernmental Panel on Climate Change (IPCC) to assess the science related to climate change. Its purpose is to inform decision-makers and provide the scientific basis for climate policy. This includes the policy negotiations under the UNFCCC (the UN's Framework Convention on Climate Change), established in 1992 to help prevent "dangerous human interference with the climate system."[13] Both the 1997 Kyoto Protocol and 2015 Paris Agreement were built on the UNFCCC. The organization also holds the acclaimed Conference of Parties—COP—to meet regularly to assess developments and set goals related to climate shifts. (More on the most recent meeting, COP28, later.)

The IPCC reports on scientific, technical, and socioeconomic impacts of climate change as well as prepares and shares guidelines for organizations and businesses related to GHG inventories. The IPCC authors report from three groups:

- **Working Group I** looks at the physical science basis of climate change.
- **Working Group II** studies the impacts of climate change and adaptation.
- **Working Group III** examines how to cut down human influence on the global climate system.

Additional task forces and groups, including experts and scientists, contribute to the reports.[14]

Rio Earth Summit

The UN Conference on Environment and Development (UNCED), also known as the Earth Summit or Rio Summit, was held in Rio de Janeiro, Brazil, in summer 1992 and brought together representatives from 179 countries, including the United States, to talk about "the impact of human socio-economic activities on the environment." Among the topics of discussion by these leaders, scientists, and experts was the effects of capitalism on climate change and where do we go from here. This was the first global treaty that explicitly addressed the issue.

Out of the discussions came a framework for sustainable development in the 21st century that addressed issues like economy, climate, and international development. It also established an annual forum—the COP—to work on stabilizing global GHGs.[15]

Though not legally binding, the Rio Summit became the catalyst for climate action and provided a broader focus to address environmental and developmental issues. To use a sports analogy, it was the opening kickoff in this global game to address the need to save the Earth as we know it. In agreeing to play, the participants chose to protect the Earth.

Kyoto Protocol

The Kyoto Protocol was the first climate treaty that was legally binding. Adopted in 1997, it went into effect in 2005, and stipulated that developed countries cut GHG emissions to an average of 5% below 1990 levels. Unfortunately, two major GHG contributors, China and India, were not compelled to cut emissions. At first the United States signed the agreement, but later withdrew its signature.[16]

Politics aside, as a global citizen, I understand both sides. On the one hand, there's urgency for emissions reduction, which we want collaboratively and harmoniously to do together. However, if the burden falls on a teammate not fully committed and with different economic fundamentals, then I don't think it's the fault of the United States for backing out to ensure that the terms of the agreement benefit both sides. Instead, we should always look for a win-win outcome.

Paris Agreement

In an effort to force countries to cut back GHG emissions, the Paris Agreement in 2015 mandated countries to pledge specific emissions-reduction targets and meet them. Those targets are known as nationally determined contributions (NDCs).

The Paris Agreement is a landmark document because, for the first time, a binding agreement was enacted to bring all nations together to combat the climate crisis. The United States initially signed the agreement during the Obama administration, then the issue turned political during the Trump administration when it withdrew support in 2017. The country rejoined the agreement in 2021 during the Biden administration.[17]

The goal of the Paris Agreement targets remains to maintain global temperature increases within the 1.5°C (2.7°F) set by scientists as necessary to stave off the worst of climate change. Further, the Paris Agreement aims to help the globe achieve net-zero emissions by 2050. That's the point where the total GHGs emitted equals the amount removed. It's estimated that to achieve the 1.5°C limit, the world will have to cut GHG emissions by 55% by 2030.

Global Warming

The Paris Agreement calls for limiting global warming to "well below 2°C relative to preindustrial temperatures, preferably to 1.5°C." These are science-based targets in line with what climate science shows are necessary to meet the goals of the Paris Agreement.

At a global warming level (GWL) of 2°C (3.6°F), the average temperature across the United States is "very likely" to increase between 4.4°F and 5.6°F (2.4°C and 3.1°C). For every additional 1°C of global warming, the average US temperature is projected to increase by about 2.5°F (1.4°C).

Source: US Global Change Research Program; Sciencebasedtargets.org.[18]

The Paris Agreement was an even more ambitious target than Kyoto and set the stage for more transparency and accountability. Countries were subjected to regular voluntary review of their progress to curb GHGs. This also was the collective action that consumers wanted from their leaders when it came to international climate efforts.

By the Numbers

As you can see, climate change, like capitalism, is about the numbers. In the business world, a company must be able to prove that it's making progress. The same is true with climate accounting and emissions reductions. Unfortunately, though, in the climate space various agencies and organizations provide different numbers, scenarios, and outcomes based on different reporting frameworks. Many of the numbers are voluntary, so organizations haven't had to disclose what they don't want to, and instead they paint a more favorable picture. That further adds to the confusion and misinformation. (I'll talk more about greenwashing—the environmental version of whitewashing—in Chapter 3.)

Nonetheless, reputable climate scientists and experts for decades have provided the world with accurate and valuable numbers to help us navigate the road to finding solutions to solving our climate crisis. Following are some numbers that can help us all, especially corporations, gain a better understanding of the challenges we face:

- In 2019, the United States emitted 5,130 million metric tons of energy-related carbon dioxide; globally the total was 33,621.5 million metric tons. (One metric ton is 2,204.6 pounds.)[19]
- To put those numbers in perspective, at standard temperature and pressure, 1 metric ton of CO_2 would fill a sphere 32 feet (about 9.8 meters) in diameter.[20]
- The social cost of carbon equals $185 per ton of CO_2 more than three times higher than the US government's 2022 value of $51 per ton of CO_2.[21]
- The good news is that global energy-related carbon dioxide emissions only rose 1.1% in 2023 to 36.8 billion metric tons.[22]
- That's a new record, but far below the gains that had been predicted.
- In not so good news, scientists—including from NASA and Columbia University—now predict Earth will exceed the 1.5°C threshold this decade. That's according to a study released in November 2023. The IPCC typically has predicted that wouldn't happen until the 2030s. The change in predictions, according to

this study, results from a better understanding of ancient climate and Earth's sensitivity to GHG emissions.[23]

Capitalistic Opportunities

All that said, there's still optimism. Capitalism, with its innovation and change, provides the perfect opportunity for profits while solving the climate dilemma. That's because profit incentivizes us. Climate solutions and the services that accompany them include everything from traditional sustainability consulting to cutting-edge AI tools that forecast weather patterns for shipping logistics, sea wall defense systems, renewable energy resources, carbon capture services, and so much more.

The next great frontier is the sustainability revolution. The challenge is so enormous for countries and companies to achieve their decarbonization goals that there will be major opportunities and new market leaders focused on addressing our climate issues. (More later on the climate tech revolution in Chapter 9.)

The Big Picture: A Chapter Roundup

- Since the Industrial Revolution, Earth's warming has been driven primarily by human activities.
- The Paris Agreement, a landmark document, is a binding agreement enacted to bring all nations together to combat the climate crisis.
- Fossil fuels like coal, natural gas, and petroleum, are hydrocarbons, meaning they are made up of primarily carbon and hydrogen. When they are combusted or burned, the oxygen combines with carbon to form CO_2 and with hydrogen to form water H_2O.
- Climate change, like capitalism, is about the numbers. Different agencies and organizations can offer different numbers, scenarios, and outcomes. Those numbers can be (and are) sometimes manipulated to meet the needs for specific outcomes.
- The opportunities for companies to profit from climate moves and adjustments are endless, whether related to discovery, innovation, adaptation, technology, mitigation, energy transition, or something completely new.

3

The Growing Power of Climate Stakeholders and Externalities

"The same capitalistic market forces that have led to environmental destruction and pollution will generate countervailing forces that promote positive climate action."

THE FOUNDATIONAL ELEMENTS of capitalist theory ignored our planet's climate. Consequently, everyone did, too, until now. That doesn't mean the days of overconsumption and convenience culture are over, but climate survival now requires us to rethink and readjust.

For centuries, the guiding principle of capitalism was profits; companies existed to create value for their stakeholders who were shareholders and owners of the companies. Profits were a moral imperative of a capitalistic society, period. More recently, however, realities and sentiments have changed. Those same market forces that perpetuated environmental destruction and pollution now are poised to have the opposite effect as populations—voluntarily or not—out of necessity have begun to care about our climate and its effect on the livability of our planet.

At its core, the causality of this capitalistic flip flop is a shift in stakeholders across much of the developed world. ESG has not yet become an important consideration in daily life in much of the lower and middle socioeconomic world. However, in the developed world, no longer are the crucial stakeholders only business owners and shareholders seeking profits. As you've read so far, much of the world has awakened to the reality that we all have a stake in maintaining a livable planet. If we can't breathe the air, lack fertile soil and clean water to grow the crops, and are unable to find a livable property in a tolerable climate, all the profits in the world matter little.

As part of its work to combat climate change, the United Nations defines stakeholders as individuals or groups who have anything of value (both monetary and nonmonetary) that might be affected by climate change or by the actions taken to manage anticipated climate risks. That includes policymakers, scientists, communities, and/or managers in the sectors and regions most at risk both now and in the future. (The UN Framework Convention on Climate Change and the Intergovernmental Panel on Climate Change were both established by the United Nations to deal with the climate crisis.)[1]

I've said it before, but it's definitely worth repeating: Inherent in the structure of capitalism are innovation and creativity. Both provide the foundation for identifying and following through on solutions to climate and environmental challenges.

Coping with Climate Externalities

Unlike their predecessors, stakeholders today have begun to pay attention to climate externalities also known broadly as sustainability. Externalities are the costs or benefits of an economic activity that aren't reflected in the market price of the goods or services. With climate, that includes everything from air, ground, and water pollution to local economic impact.

A negative externality is the factory that pollutes the air as a by-product of its production process. Without any regulation and enforcement, by the Environmental Protection Agency in the United States, for example, the cost of the pollution isn't reflected in the price of the factory's products so the factory has no financial incentive to reduce its pollution.

There is a price we pay for that negative externality. Between 2010 and 2020, highly vulnerable regions of the world, home to approximately 3.3 to 3.6 billion people, experienced 15 times higher human mortality rates from floods, droughts, and storms compared with regions with very low vulnerability.[2] These negative externalities affect our livelihoods.

Since the 1980s, climate-related events—including higher temperatures and intensified weather events—cost the European Union almost $534 billion in financial losses. More than 138,000 people died due to extreme weather and climate-related events between 1980 and 2020.[3]

Externalities also can be positive. For example, a farmer plants trees on part of their land; those trees then provide various benefits to society like cleaning the air, creating wildlife habitat, and preventing soil erosion. However, these benefits aren't reflected in the market price of the wheat the farmer grows, so the farmer doesn't have a financial incentive to plant more trees.

In a capitalist economy, externalities can lead to market failure because the market does not accurately reflect the costs and benefits of economic activities. A monopoly, for example, could be a market failure because prices are set regardless of supply and demand. Or, the air-polluting factory has no incentive to limit production—or pollution—and that leads to overproduction of the goods because the factory has an incentive to produce as much as possible to maximize profits. All the while, the costs of pollution are being passed on to society as a whole.

As with the clean air and water acts discussed in Chapter 2, governments can intervene to internalize externalities with the help of regulations, taxes, or subsidies to shore up markets or encourage more socially optimal outcomes. For example, federal, state, and local governments across the United States as well as countries around the globe encourage purchase of electric vehicles to curb greenhouse gas (GHG) emissions. These government entities offer broad financial incentives to drastically reduce necessary individual financial outlays.

As capitalism evolves further, it will take into account more of these externalities at scale across global markets and become the key driver in solving the climate crisis. Countries or localities, for example, could levy taxes designed to discourage/encourage a particular behavior and/or pay for the cost of the negative externalities associated with driving.

Currently in the United States, the federal taxes levied on gasoline are an example of this—what's known as a *Pigouvian tax*. Another Pigouvian tax is France's noise tax levied at its 10 busiest airports. Unfortunately, these taxes simply become a way of life and not a deterrent.[4] Maybe in the future that will change if the financial cost is high enough.

Capitalism Enhancements

To better understand why massive increases in air pollution led to and still drive shifts in our climate and public opinion, we need to again look back at how the tenets of capitalism incentivized earlier stakeholders.

Market Economy

Adam Smith, often called the father of modern economics,[5] discussed the concept of a market economy and the principles of economic liberalism in his 1776 book, *The Wealth of Nations*. The most efficient and fair way to organize an economy, wrote Smith, is through the free market. Further, that free market, operating according to the principles of supply and demand, would naturally lead to the most efficient allocation of resources and the greatest level of economic growth.

Financial profit, Smith said, was a natural and necessary component of a market economy that serves as an incentive for entrepreneurs to *innovate* and *create* new products and services that meet the needs and desires of consumers. Smith also recognized that profit can sometimes be the result of monopolistic practices or other forms of market failure. In such cases, he believed that government intervention might be necessary to correct such problems and to ensure that the market is operating efficiently. All of this figures into how capitalism will be the driver in the context of finding solutions to our climate crisis.

More recently, 20th-century Nobel Prize–winning economist Milton Friedman took Smith's teachings about the importance of profits a step further. "There is one and only one social responsibility of business—to use its resources and engage in activities designed to increase its profits so long as it stays within the rules of the game, which is to say, engages in open and free competition without deception or fraud," Friedman wrote in a September 1970 *New York Times* essay.[6]

Friedman argued that profits were not only a necessary part of a healthy market economy but also a way for businesses to serve the needs and interests of their customers and to contribute to the overall well-being of society. He believed that businesses had a moral obligation to act in the best interests of their shareholders and to generate profits, as long as they did so in a way that was consistent with the principles of a free market.

Friedman also said that externalities could be addressed through government regulations or taxes, which could internalize the costs or benefits of an economic activity and help correct market failures. However, he emphasized that government intervention should be limited and that the market should be allowed to function as freely as possible.

Unfortunately, that freedom can create conflict and damage in the interim as governments usually act retroactively, rather than proactively, to market developments for a variety of reasons. The catch-up game governments engage in today when it comes to our climate is an excellent example of this in action.

A Livable Planet

With the teachings of Smith and Friedman in mind, an inhabitable planet likely ranks high on the list of necessary elements to ensure a viable economic system in the best interests of society over the long term. Nonetheless, until very recently our planet's health and biodiversity simply were nonfactors unless they related to access to natural resources or the viability of operations. Both have economic value in a capitalist system.

Natural resources include both renewable resources, which can be replenished over time, and nonrenewable ones, which are finite and will eventually be depleted. Wind, for example, is a renewable resource; oil and wildlife, once depleted or extinct, are gone and can't be replenished.

Historically societies, governments, and businesses only factored in natural resources and environmental factors as they pertained to direct and generally short-term economic impact. To be fair, people didn't realize or recognize that coastlines would disappear or that certain regions of the planet would become uninhabitable due to extreme heat and changes in severe weather patterns. At most, people historically factored in environmental destruction as a nuisance that required new economic infrastructure to compensate. People simply did not consider the ramifications of GHGs and their long-term negative effects on our planet.

Supply and Demand

By its very nature, capitalism creates winners and losers. The big winners of the past have been private enterprises and their shareholders; the losers, society and our planet, its land, seas, and air.

As GHGs in the atmosphere add up and awareness of climate change grows, though, so do the number of stakeholders who want solutions to the crisis. With those added stakeholders come government and societal checks and balances, with the help of capitalism, innovation, and creativity to solve challenges.

For example, when those out-of-control record-breaking Canadian wildfires fouled the air as far south as Washington, DC, and beyond in summer 2023, they also sent a clear message that something must be done to stem the climate crisis. The wildfires were the most destructive ever recorded in Canada, their severity fanned by the state of the climate.[7]

Why were 2023's Canadian wildfires such a wake-up call? Beyond their sheer size and intensity, the fires hit capitalism's bottom line—profits—well beyond Canada's southern border. The extreme particulate pollution over much of the United States that summer not only fouled the air, clouded the sun, and choked all in its path but also forced schools, organizations, and businesses to cancel activities. Outdoor professional sports teams had to cancel games; outdoor and indoor workers were sent home; performances—including on Broadway in New York City—were canceled; and billions of dollars lost. That's in addition to the billions of dollars in direct cost of the fires in Canada.

More important, the world watched and heard it all in minute detail thanks to our interconnected, social media—hungry world.

Climate Propaganda

With idea sharing via the internet and social media as close as your phone or smart speaker, talk of climate shifts—good and bad—spreads quickly. Disseminating misinformation, misdirections, and blatant lies is as easy as spreading the crucial truth.

Often it's tough to differentiate between what's right and what isn't. Spin these days is everything and everywhere.

The vast majority of people finally believe that climate change is real. After all, it's tough to dispute something so prevalent in all our lives. Nonetheless there are still holdouts. About 10% of the US population today deny climate change exists despite the science behind it, says Michael Mann, US climatologist, geophysicist, and director of the Center for Science, Sustainability & the Media, at the University of Pennsylvania. He's also author of *Our Fragile Moment: How Lessons from Earth's Past Can Help Us Survive the Climate Crisis*.[8]

There are the dismissers and downplayers, says Mann. These are people who grudgingly admit climate is changing but downplay its negative effects. Often that means perpetuating misleading climate propaganda.

Big oil and gas companies are notorious for their climate talk or lack thereof. As a brief example, consider one of those people caught in the fray, Rex Tillerson, former US Secretary of State and the former CEO of ExxonMobil, 2006–2016. According to a *Wall Street Journal* report, "The effort to minimize concerns about climate change under former chief executive Rex Tillerson . . . was happening at the same time that scientists at the company were modeling troubling increases in carbon dioxide emissions without big reductions in fossil fuel consumption."[9]

The State of New York even brought charges against Exxon for misleading the public about the dangers of climate change, but they eventually lost the case. Various government and private entities also have taken Exxon and other oil and gas companies to task, accusing them of downplaying the effects of fossil fuels on the environment and climate change in general.[10]

Some of those cases have had more success in the courts than the Exxon case. In 2021, for example, a Dutch court in The Hague ordered Royal Dutch Shell to cut CO_2 emissions by 45% relative to

2019 levels by 2030 after it was found guilty of misleading consumers on its emissions.[11]

Greenwashing

Organizations like Royal Dutch Shell mislead consumers via *greenwashing*, creating a false impression or inflating environmental action through misinformation. The term *greenwash* is a play on the word *whitewash*, which means to cover up poor or unlawful behavior through biased data, intentional misrepresentation, and other means.[12]

False Advertising

Governments take greenwashing very seriously no matter who does it and in what context. In 2022 mega retailers Walmart and Kohl's faced hefty fines by the US Federal Trade Commission for false advertising related to sustainability. The retailers advertised sustainable "bamboo" pajamas, but the pajamas were actually made of rayon, a semisynthetic fiber. In accordance with a settlement, Kohl's had to pay $2.5 million and Walmart $3 million in civil penalties. That might be a drop in the bucket for the retailing behemoths, but it's also a wake-up call that there are standards and regulations surrounding sustainability claims that must be adhered to.[13]

Many people likely remember another mega case of greenwashing involving air pollution and auto manufacturer Volkswagen AG. In the mid-2000s, Volkswagen marketed its "environmentally friendly" diesel vehicles, claiming they had lower carbon dioxide emissions and better fuel efficiency. It turned out the company had installed software on its cars to enable them to cheat US emission tests and appear less polluting than they actually were. Martin Winterkorn, the former chairman of the management board of Volkswagen AG, was charged with conspiracy and wire fraud in connection with the scheme.[14]

Over the years, greenwashing tactics have become more sophisticated. As pressure from public stakeholders has mounted, companies have begun using research creatively to appear greener than they are.

The bottom line is that greenwashing has to stop. We are right now at the make or break point to save our climate and maintain a livable planet.

"In practice, fossil fuel companies, airlines, and car brands employ misleading labels or advertising campaigns to show a faux commitment to net-zero ambitions and to depict themselves as being climate conscious without transforming their business models, which caused the climate crisis in the first place," writes Zeina Moneer for the Middle East Institute.[15]

Carbon Offsets

Greenwashing comes in many forms including carbon offsets, which are popular and seem positive to the general public. A carbon offset is a right that companies or individuals can purchase and trade to offset or account for their GHG emissions into the atmosphere. A company, for example, can comply with emissions caps by buying carbon credits from an independent organization. The organization will then use that money to fund a project that reduces carbon in the atmosphere. A renewable energy project could include protecting forests or improving the energy efficiency of a building.

Remember that the term *carbon* can be used as a catch-all for GHGs in general. An individual can also engage with this system and similarly pay to offset their own personal carbon use instead of, or in addition to, taking direct measures such as driving less or recycling.

The ABCs of Carbon

- **Carbon credits.** *Also known as carbon allowances, these are tradable permits or certificates that represent the offset of one ton of carbon dioxide equivalent (CO_2e) emissions.*
- **Carbon markets.** *Public and private marketplaces where carbon credits are bought and sold.*
- **Carbon offsets.** *The use of carbon credits to offset the amount of carbon that an individual or institution emits into the*

(*continued*)

(continued)

atmosphere; can be bought and retired by individuals or companies to balance their own emissions.

- **Carbon offtake.** Direct removal and sequestering of CO_2 from the air; sequestration can be permanently underground or by technological means.

Most offsets involve renewable energy. For example, a company in Massachusetts can pay to build a wind turbine off the coast. By using its money to create renewable energy, that company thereby offsets its own carbon use.

The drawback with this approach is that companies or institutions often use carbon offsets to reduce their carbon footprint without polluting less. Polluting corporations like airlines rely on carbon offsetting to reduce emissions—from flights, for example—they can't currently cut down.

Offsetting claims also can go awry when companies rely on low-quality or unverified projects that don't actually remove or avoid carbon emissions as claimed. This results in unmet goals and misrepresented progress, which is harmful to businesses, stakeholders, and the environment.

Legal actions related to misleading and even false statements and advertising are a who's who among the world's leading airlines. In one typical case, the UK's Advertising Standards Authority zeroed in on Ireland-based Ryanair for running commercials in 2019 that claimed they were the lowest-emissions airline in Europe. That moniker, the air carrier claimed, was based on studies and data they had completed. The ASA ruled against Ryanair, and ordered the ads removed, saying they were misleading and violated the UK Code of Non-broadcast Advertising, Sales Promotion and Direct Marketing.[16]

"It's no news that legacy carriers have enjoyed preferential treatment under EU climate measures," says Jo Dardenne, aviation manager at Transport & Environment, a European clean transport nonprofit. "They make crowd-pleasing pledges of net-zero emissions, which is music to the ears of their investors and customers. But in the background, they send IAG (International Airlines Group) and IATA (International Air Transport Association) to do

their dirty work: lobby to weaken the EU's climate package so they can continue to pollute for free."[17]

Data Integrity

Clearly there's an issue of trust in people, data, and claims in the ESG or sustainability space today. People prioritize climate, but navigating information related to sustainability is challenging. A recent industry survey highlighted a lack of trust in corporate sustainability reporting, with over 75% of respondents concerned about the accuracy of the information.[18]

Companies must look to enhance corporate data, systems, governance practice, alongside the development of a globally consistent reporting and assurance standard to build trust in the sustainability efforts.

Accurate Environmental Data

That distrust and lack of global standards has not gone unnoticed. As corporate environmental performance gains more scrutiny and becomes more closely linked to economic performance, regulators recognize the need for more accurate environmental data. That's especially pertinent to stakeholders and investors as more sustainability issues move further into the courts.

Accurate and verifiable data, like measurements of GHG emissions or carbon accounting, are essential; lack of standard procedures and inconsistent evidence simply aren't enough anymore. That's where technology and standardized practices have begun to fill the void. The need for broadly accepted standards specific to sustainability is a cornerstone to overcoming the climate crisis.

The SASB (Sustainability Standards Board; www.SASB.org) and the ISSB (International Sustainability Standards Board), both arms of the IFRS (International Financial Reporting Standards), are nonprofit industry organizations that create industry-based standards—benchmarks—to help companies identify and disclose financially material sustainability information. Those standards can help companies identify sustainability opportunities and risks as well as the right metrics to use in their disclosures.[19] As of August 2022, ISSB assumed responsibility for the SASB standards.

Issuing its inaugural global sustainability standards in June 2023, the newly combined group said, "for the first time, the standards create a common language for disclosing the effect of climate-related risks and opportunities on a company's prospects."[20]

Simply put and well said.

Countries and their governments are taking notice, too. A number of laws and organizations address this seemingly broad campaign of accuracy and transparency associated with climate and sustainability. Here is some of what's happening around the globe:

- **US Securities and Exchange Commission.** Its climate risk disclosure rule will help guarantee that companies accurately measure their GHG emissions and report relevant climate risks and opportunities.[21]
- **US Federal Trade Commission's Green Guides.** These aren't legally binding, but they provide guidance to help marketers avoid making misleading environmental claims.[22]
- **European Union's Sustainable Finance Disclosure Regulation.** This transparency framework spells out how companies have to disclose substantive sustainability-related financial information.[23]
- **EU's Green Claims Directive.** This policy will include standardized methodologies companies must use to substantiate any "green claims."[24]
- **France's Climate and Resilience Law.** This prohibits claims of carbon neutrality unless the company can provide specific evidence to support that claim.[25]
- **European Securities and Markets Authority (ESMA) Sustainable Finance Roadmap 2022–2024.** This prioritizes promoting transparency and tackling greenwashing during this period by providing guidance for supervising investment funds with sustainability features.[26]

Marriage of Capitalism and Sustainability

As capitalism and sustainability come together, companies, organizations, and governments also join hands to identify, address, and solve Earth's climate challenges. Harnessing market forces, these public-private partnerships are spurring breakthrough advancements in renewable energy, creating green jobs, and fostering sustainable communities.

These partnerships usher in major periods of technological and economic advancement, as well as conflict. History most certainly repeats itself, albeit in different forms, and the response of governments and private industry alike to the climate crisis will result in yet another cycle of creation and destruction in the decades to come.

A shift in power from manufacturing-based economies to consumer- and service-oriented ones will ultimately lead to a shift back to the former due to the never-ending global appetite for consumption.

When there is a rebalancing and a shift of power, though, there will always be conflict. In the worst cases, these will result in physical conflicts and sometimes all-out war. Legacy corporations will work to stifle disruptive technologies and business models just as the oil and gas industry and the automotive industry have done in recent decades.

And, as mentioned previously, as is a tenet of capitalism, there will be winners and losers. That can be positive for our climate because high-polluting industries and nations need to begin losing market share and influence in favor of those that are initially less carbon intensive on the environment and ultimately regenerative.

Geopolitics in the Mix

Geopolitical ramifications of the climate crisis are a natural outgrowth of the winners and losers in the capitalism scenario. Russia's invasion of Ukraine in 2022, for example, posed a threat economically and politically to Europe because of the region's dependence on Russian natural gas and oil. Of the 10.1 million barrels per day of crude oil and condensate that Russia produced in 2021, the country exported more than 45%, the majority of it to Europe. The Netherlands and Germany alone combined received 1.1 million barrels of oil a day from Russia.[27]

As with crude oil and condensates exports, Europe was the largest regional importer of Russia's natural gas, accounting for nearly 75% of Russia's total natural gas exports or almost 6.6 trillion cubic feet.[28]

These complicated economic and energy ties between Russia and the EU have led to Russia using its energy exports as a political tool.

Beyond upsetting the politics, upending these markets can have a negative impact on attempts to curtail GHGs. Consider that within Europe, Germany was the biggest importer of Russian natural gas, accounting for more than a third of the country's total gas consumption. The use of natural gas has helped Germany migrate away from coal and nuclear power, thus playing a key role in the country's efforts to decarbonize its energy sector.

To reduce its dependence on Russian gas and strengthen its energy security, the EU has sought to diversify its energy sources as it transitions away from fossil fuels. That includes increased use of renewables as well as finding other sources to meet its energy needs. Various countries also have invested in infrastructure to import gas from other countries, like Norway and Algeria. The EU also worked to improve the transparency and security of its gas supply through the establishment of the Single European Gas Market.

This is just one example of winner-loser scenarios in the future context of how the climate crisis will spur resource shortages that will significantly affect modern life. One certainty, though, is that today's and future definitions of winning include protecting and fixing our climate.

A Shortage of Talent

Adding to the challenges, as we move from a voluntary to regulated reporting environment, corporations are forced to ramp up their staff dedicated to sustainability, reporting, and compliance. Unfortunately, that's a tough task considering the shortage of talent with the right expertise. Nearly 70% of publicly traded US-headquartered companies named internal controls over sustainability reporting as a skill they need to fill right now, according to a recent study from the Financial Education & Research Foundation.[29]

With the SEC's recent rule adoption to enhance and standardize climate-related disclosures for investors, many public companies will be required to report their GHG Scope 1 and 2 emissions with phase-in assurance verification. SEC Chair Gary Gensler states, "The rules will provide investors with consistent, comparable, and decision-useful information."[30] As companies prepare for their first mandated climate disclosures, internal audit and governance teams are scrambling to review climate related risks and controls and verifying climate data-integrity given the risk of SEC violations. And it's made more difficult because sustainability data—including GHG emissions—isn't confined to one segment of any company. Instead, it spreads across the entire organization and the supply chain.

We see a prevalence of financial accounting experts. However, carbon accounting requires the ability to track, search for the data details, then measure, and calculate. That's a unique skill set that's necessary even with the right software, automation, and artificial intelligence tools to help.

The Big Picture: A Chapter Roundup

- Climate survival requires us to rethink and readjust how we view capitalism. Profits remain tantamount with considerations to new externalities. However, climate no longer is an obscure long-term threat. Climate change costs businesses and consumers money now, and those costs will only escalate.

- Historically, people only factored in natural resources and environmental factors as they pertained to direct and generally short-term economic impact. A resource shortage was a nuisance. But then almost no one realized their actions could make parts of our planet uninhabitable due to extreme heat and changes in severe weather patterns.

- Greenwashing, the environmental equivalent of whitewashing, has been a prevalent force in climate discussions and debates over the decades. Studies show investor trust is an issue in the ESG space with today's "difficult" information environment.

- Accurate and verifiable data, like measurements of GHGs or CO_2 emissions, are essential.

- The SASB and the ISSB, both arms of the IFRS, are nonprofit industry organizations that create industry-based standards—benchmarks—to help companies identify and disclose financially material sustainability information.

- Geopolitical ramifications of the climate crisis are a natural outgrowth of the winners and losers in the capitalism scenario.

Think about the European Union's dependence on Russian oil and gas prior to Russia's invasion of Ukraine.
- With the SEC's recent rule adoption to enhance and standardize climate-related disclosures for investors, many public companies will be required to report their GHG Scope 1 and 2 emissions with phase-in assurance verification.

4

Fossil Fuels

Culprit or Savior or Both

"Capitalism creates winners and losers. Win-win scenarios are rare."

TO BE CRYSTAL clear, the fossil fuel industry did not cause the record levels of greenhouse gases (GHGs) in our atmosphere. A consumer-based economy with insatiable need to grow is to blame. After all, the fossil fuel industry wouldn't exist without demand for its products—coal, oil/petroleum, and natural gas being the most notable.

Putting aside the negative aspects of burning fossil fuels, these minerals utterly changed the world. The energy industry touches nearly every aspect of our lives. Almost everything we consume, everything we transport, and everything we build requires energy to do so. Such is the critical nuance of the role the fossil fuel industry plays in the broader story of our climate.

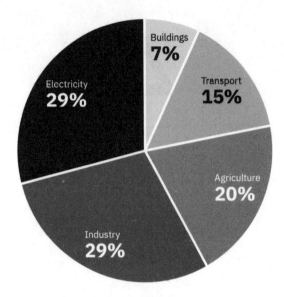

Figure 4.1   Global emissions by sector

Note: Percentage share of 2021 net GHG emissions.

Dominant in Our Lives

Beyond the electricity in our homes and the gasoline in our cars, fossil fuels have their fingerprints on so much, from the food we eat to the clothes we wear (see Figure 4.1). Consider some of the ways people use fossil fuels globally:

- **Electricity generation.** Especially coal and natural gas to heat and power homes and buildings.
- **Industrial processes.** Used in feedstocks and in the production of a variety of chemicals and products; natural gas, for example, is used to produce ammonia, which is used in the production of fertilizers and other products.
- **Plastics.** Plays a crucial role in their creation and is in everything from shopping bags to water bottles and children's toys.
- **Asphalt and paving materials.** Requires petroleum products for their production.
- **Lubricants.** Uses oil to produce lubricants for a variety of applications.

- **Medicines.** Uses petrochemicals in the production of or are in certain medications, including lubricants, creams, ointments, and gels.
- **Pesticides.** Used in the production and management of crops.
- **Personal care products.** In the production of some personal care products like makeup and shampoo.

Beyond the Basics

To further clarify how pervasive fossil fuels are in our lives and their role in our shifting climate, here's a breakdown of global GHG emissions by sector (as a percentage share of 2021 net GHG emissions, according to data consultants the Rhodium Group:

- **Buildings.** 7% total (residential 4%, commercial 1%, refrigerants 2%).
- **Transport.** 15% total (roads 12%, ships 2%, aviation 1%).
- **Agriculture, land use, and waste.** 20% total (livestock 7%, crops 6%, landfills and waste 4%, land use and forests 2%, agriculture fuel combustion less than 1%).
- **Industry.** 29% total (oil and gas 6%, iron and steel 5%, cement 5%, chemicals 4%, coal mining 2%, refining 1%, other industries 7%).
- **Electricity.** 29% total (coal 21%, natural gas 7%, oil 1%).[1]

As the numbers reflect, a big share of global emissions can be attributed to the energy sector of our economy. In 2021, fossil fuels accounted for 79% of primary energy use in the United States. The remaining energy was provided by renewables including wind, biofuels, hydro, and others.[2]

Dive deeper into the data, however, and you see that fossil fuel producers are not the main source of GHG emissions. Rather, it is the use of the products they bring to market—our consumerism. That's why identifying alternate forms of energy is vital to a sustainable economy. Solutions can include electrification, carbon neutral power, carbon neutral hydrogen fuel, feedstocks as fuel, and so much more. Greater energy efficiency and circularity also are essential. (I'll talk more about some of those alternate sources of energy in Chapter 10.)

Two Sides to the Argument

For some people, this is where the philosophical debate begins on who is responsible for the climate crisis. Is it consumerism or the fossil fuel energy industry? Since these conversations began, people are quick to cast aspersions against the fossil fuel industry. But, it's important to note there are merits to both sides of the argument.

Fossil fuels in and of themselves are not inherently good or bad; neither is the use of them. They are similar to technology in that sense; they are simply resources that can be applied both ways. What cannot be argued, however, is that fossil fuels are vital to life as we know it and will be for a long time.

As a participant past and present, I've experienced multiple sides of the fossil fuel and climate equation. I have learned it's inappropriate to paint the fossil fuel industry or the environmental activists with a broad brushstroke. The realities of individual situations differ whether the accuser or defendant comes from the far left, far right, or somewhere in between.

Coal companies, for example, in many ways are synonymous with climate shifts and environmental destruction. But coal miners themselves aren't taking on the burden of that dangerous and hard work they perform each day with the express purpose of damaging our planet. They're not participating in some master plan to make themselves rich or to exploit others. These people earn an honest living to support their families. I have witnessed firsthand the truly impressive work ethic, resilience, and family-oriented ethos that define so many people in that industry.

I have also been a participant in the corporate theater of big energy companies and witnessed what happens and why. That includes shareholder pressure on companies to become more transparent in terms of carbon emissions. This is where capitalism and its pursuit of profits reenters the climate equation. The prospect of profits has always been a powerful corruptor, and when you add the phenomenal scale and size of profits possible in an industry as big and rich as the oil and gas industry, capitalism creates the perfect recipe for disaster.

This is no different than any other industry on the planet. Where there is money to be made, there will be bad actors. The oil and gas industry is often naively painted as the primary culprit of the climate crisis. While the industry has a role to fulfill, the people of the industry don't actively set out to destroy the planet. Many people I've met in the industry are hard-working, honest workers, entrepreneurs who ensure the availability of energy for all else. That being said, there's no question that the industry has, and continues to play a role in the systematic cover-up and obfuscation of the impacts of fossil fuels on climate and outright climate denialism.

Follow the Facts

The last sentence uses strong words, but they're backed up by the facts. There's more, too, that goes well beyond misinformation campaigns.

As a former oil and gas industry C-suite executive, I've witnessed powerful and wealthy leaders not only deny the science but publicly mock the concept of climate change. I've also seen those same elite individuals pressured by shareholders to divulge climate truths.

What's the Truth?

Though the fossil fuel industry isn't responsible for alterations to our climate, as a whole, there's no question it has perpetuated the global rhetoric and denialism. The oil and gas industry unequivocally knew about climate change, GHGs, and their effect on our climate, air, and seas for decades. That's a truth supported by well-established research from reputable groups ranging from colleges and universities to climate scientists, investigative journalists, and even scientists working for big oil themselves.

This was a decades-long well-coordinated and well-funded effort intended to deceive the American people (and the world) about changing climate realities, according to Justin Farrell, in testimony to the US Senate Special Committee on the Climate Crisis in October 2019. Farrell is a sociology professor at Yale's School of Environment and author of several books and articles on the environment.[3]

Dispelling Any Doubts

In case someone doubts the words of a professor, consider what J. F. Black, an expert in Exxon's products research and engineering division, reported to his company as far back as 1977:

> *The Greenhouse Effect . . . The Earth's atmosphere presently contains about 330 ppm of CO_2. This gas does not absorb an appreciable amount of the incoming solar energy but it can absorb and return part of the infrared radiation (heat) which the earth radiates toward space. CO_2 therefore, contributes to warming the lower atmosphere by what has been called the Greenhouse Effect . . . studies show that CO_2 is increasing. If the increase is attributed to the combustion of fossil fuels, it can be calculated then that the CO_2 content of the atmosphere has already been raised by about 10 to 15% and that slightly more than half of the CO_2 released by fossil fuel combustion is remaining in the atmosphere . . . This growth curve is close to that predicted by Exxon's Corporate Planning Department.*[4]

Black goes on to address global warming and melting polar ice caps as a result of these GHGs.

More Proof

The evidence of the early culpability of big oil's coverup is broad and unquestionable. It goes well beyond Farrell's testimony and Black's presentation, or accusations of greenwashing.

Here's a sampling of a few of the literally hundreds of headlines over the years:

- **"BP Acknowledged Climate Risk of Fossil Fuels in 1990"** (Center for International Environmental Law). "Dutch think tank Changerism and investigative platform Follow the Money released a new expose on 'What Makes Weather?' a recently unearthed climate video produced by BP in 1990 . . . Despite this knowledge (of the climate risks of fossil fuels) as documented by Changerism and others, BP spent the next three decades obstructing meaningful climate action while dramatically expanding its production of fossil fuels . . ."[5]

- **"Dirty Pearls: Exposing Shell's Hidden Legacy of Climate Change Accountability, 1970–1990"** (Changerism, 2020). This "independent, in-depth research and analysis project of Changerism . . . shows that throughout the 1970s and 1980s Shell structurally developed in-house knowledge about global warming . . . Vatan Hüzeir, founder and director of Changerism: Although these first articles refer to only 38 of the many more documents amassed for *Dirty pearls*, they tell the story of Shell having engaged in what I call 'climate change uncertaintism' and 'climate change negligence.'"[6]
- **"Peabody Energy's Unprecedented Support for Climate Denial"** (NRDC, June 17, 2016). "This week, researchers confirmed that Peabody Energy, the world's largest private-sector coal company, has been funding dozens of climate denial groups, including the 'Dr. Evil' mastermind behind a number of vicious, over-the-top attacks against the Environmental Protection Agency and the Clean Power Plan. The latest revelations from Peabody's bankruptcy court documents show the unprecedented extent to which big polluters like Peabody went to subvert climate action . . ."[7]

The revelations, investigations, and exposes on big energy's climate-change coverups, accidentally on purpose oversights, and misinformation campaigns are exhaustive. For those who still cast doubt on their veracity, Google "climate change" and "oil and gas industry" or "coal industry." The results likely will shock you.

Perhaps, if the oil and gas industry had been more upfront about fossil fuels and the climate crisis, we would have been able to already have in place substantial changes in energy governance and not be dealing with a dire outlook for our planet. But hindsight doesn't solve today's climate problems. It does serve as a lesson for the future on the importance of acting now to pursue green energy solutions.

On the Positive Side

It's not all bad news, though, in terms of energy companies today addressing climate issues. Duke Energy Florida, for example, announced plans for an end-to-end system in Volusia County, Florida, that can produce, store, and combust 100% green hydrogen and will use existing solar facilities.

"Duke Energy anticipates hydrogen could play a major role in our clean energy future," said Regis Repko, senior vice president of generation and transmission strategy for Duke Energy. "Hydrogen has significant potential for decarbonization across all sectors of the U.S. economy. It is a clean energy capable of long-duration storage, which would help Duke Energy ensure grid reliability as we continue adding more renewable energy sources to our system."

ExxonMobil is moving into the energy transition space, too. In November 2023, the oil and gas giant announced an all-stock $4.9 billion deal to buy Denbury Inc., a carbon solutions company focused on the development of enhanced oil recovery, carbon capture, utilization, and storage.[8] That follows announcements earlier in the year to buy properties and produce lithium for lithium-ion batteries in Arkansas and Oklahoma.[9]

The lithium deal represents a small investment for ExxonMobil today but could mean much more as the world moves toward a greener, more electric future, says Jennifer Grancio, CEO of Engine No. 1, an impact-focused US investment firm committed to making positive sustainable changes to companies from within. The company made headlines in 2021 when as a minority shareholder in ExxonMobil it successfully spearheaded the replacement of three board members to among other things "implement a strategic plan for sustainable value creation in a decarbonizing world."[10]

BP also has committed to increasing its net renewable energy-generating capacity to 50 gigawatts by 2030, up from just 3.3 GW in 2021. The company has pledged to achieve net zero by 2050. The company is growing its electric vehicle (EV) charging stations network and expanding its solar and offshore wind energy facilities.[11]

Not So Straightforward Journey

Actually, dozens of large fossil-fuel-related publicly listed companies have agreed to the net zero 2050 target (114 according to the 2023 Net Zero Stocktake Report that tracks net-zero progress.) Hundreds of other companies globally (929 to be exact) have pledged to be net zero by 2050. But, as of June 2023, the Stocktake Report found few actually have solid plans in place to achieve that goal.[12]

That lack of actual action is consistent with what we often see from big companies—big pledges made without any clear strategy to meet those promises. It's an alarming trend because many are publicly traded and have a duty to not mislead investors and consumers. One plausible explanation is that CEOs make these pledges for 20 to 25 years in the future and simply pass the green baton to the next CEO, instead of taking action today.

The pursuit of green energy, however, also raises its own issues. Despite their intentions, green infrastructure might also lead to environmental problems like habitat or biodiversity loss, pollution, disruption in animal migration patterns, and introduction of invasive species.

With fossil fuels used directly and indirectly in so many aspects of our lives, it doesn't mean achieving net zero, as in cutting carbon emissions, is impossible. It simply means the journey will be long and full of trial and error as we seek out the best strategies to decarbonize. There are no silver bullets to solving the crisis. But we can as global citizens make progress one step and one company at a time.

Crucial Interdependencies

Before someone decides to simply bash energy companies, immediately eliminate heavy CO_2-emitting industrial companies, and shut down environmentally unfriendly operations, think again. Beyond our consumerism and pursuit of profits, so many aspects of our capitalistic economy are deeply intertwined.

The solutions to our climate issues won't happen overnight, and we need these industrial companies to support the transition to a more sustainable economy. Lithium mining, for example, takes incredible amounts of energy and pollutes the air and water, yet lithium-ion batteries currently are a crucial component in the transition to more sustainable energy sources. Lithium batteries are manufactured to power EVs and aid in the storage of wind and solar-produced energy, among other things.

Even a large-scale shift to EVs won't solve the climate crisis, either. The move is necessary to cut down on CO_2 emissions, but by itself, it's not sufficient, says Alexandre Milovanoff, a University of Toronto researcher and one of the authors of a report examining the impact of EVs on climate change that appeared in the publication *Nature Climate Change*.[13]

A massive shift to EVs also would create additional problems, including stress on the power grid to generate enough electricity to power those vehicles. That likely would require some fossil fuel—generated power. Also, as mentioned, EVs rely on lithium-ion batteries, which create their own environmental impact. They require the mining of critical minerals for production, and disposal can be problematic in terms of their flammability and toxicity.[14]

Any successful energy transition to a more sustainable economy also will require interim solutions. So, bashing the fossil fuel industry won't get us there. Instead, it will take collective efforts on the part of all stakeholders to make progress.

The Big Picture: A Chapter Roundup

- The fossil fuel industry did not cause the record levels of GHGs in our atmosphere. Consumerism is to blame.
- Fossil fuels have their fingerprints on nearly every aspect of our lives, from the foods we eat to the clothes we wear. Without them, we likely wouldn't enjoy the comforts we have today.
- In 2021, fossil fuels accounted for 79% of primary energy use in the United States.[15]
- Some in the oil and gas industry—certainly not everyone—have been guilty of obfuscation of the truth about how the burning of fossil fuels affects our environment.
- J. F. Black, an expert in Exxon's products research and engineering division, reported to his company as far back as 1977 about the greenhouse effect, CO_2's role, global warming, and more.[16]
- Any real solution to the climate crisis will be multipronged and require all of us to work together.
- Dozens of large fossil-fuel-related publicly listed companies have agreed to the net-zero 2050 target, 114 according to the 2023 Net Zero Stocktake Report that tracks net-zero progress. As of June 2023, the report found few actually have solid plans in place to achieve that goal.[17]

5

The Supply and Demand Dilemma

Short- Versus Long-Term Gains

"Sustainability has realigned power and redefined progress for the twenty-first century."

CLIMATE RISK IS financial risk. Capitalist consumerism, after all, relies on the law of supply and demand to drive markets as opposed to state planned or centralized control. And, when supplies or demands become disrupted, markets stress and profits can suffer.

There are exceptions. Manipulating supplies, for example, can push prices upward. Oil is a prime example. The Organization of Petroleum Exporting Countries (OPEC) sets production targets for member countries with the goal of managing oil pricing. If OPEC cuts production targets, crude oil prices usually climb, and vice versa, though there are exceptions to that, because not all OPEC members pay attention to production targets all the time.

Historically OPEC has occasionally used this tactic for geopolitical gains. For example, after the United States provided a chunk of emergency aid to Israel in 1973 following the Yom Kippur War with its neighbors, OPEC instituted an oil embargo on the United States. Oil was in short supply, and its price nearly quadrupled.[1] More recently, in

April 2023, OPEC cut production levels for what some believe was retaliation against the United States for its support of Ukraine in its war with Russia.[2]

The organization gets away with this pricing manipulation because its 13-member countries produce about 40% of the world's crude oil and its oil exports make up about 60% of all the petroleum traded globally.[3]

The Greening of the World

That said, even OPEC isn't immune to capitalism's winners and losers. In the 1980s, as consumers began to shift away from hydrocarbons, demand for fossil-fuel-generated energy fell and OPEC admitted times were tough. "OPEC's share of the smaller oil market fell heavily and its total petroleum revenue dropped, causing economic instability in many Member Countries," OPEC reported at the time.[4]

Of course, capitalism's economic super engine eventually returned to full power and with it the demand for energy. Oil markets, including OPEC, roared back, prices soared, and except for occasional blips, continue their upward climb to this day.

Change is happening again today, though, as the public worries about oil dependencies and our changing climate. On the insistence of consumers—market demands—sustainability has become a power shifter in our 21st-century push to save our climate.

On the micro level, individuals want action on climate issues. Boardrooms, governments, and investor groups are listening and reacting. As you read in the last chapter, legacy companies like ExxonMobil and BP, as well as others, have taken steps toward sustainability and invested in alternative energy sources in response to their stakeholders' sentiments. Only time will tell if these energy giants are truly committed to making a difference and follow through on their promises and commitments.

Other investor groups also take climate shifts seriously. Remember Engine No. 1 from Chapter 4, which took on ExxonMobil and forced a change in its board of directors? Norges Bank Investment Management is another powerful money manager that has acted on climate issues.

"Climate risk is financial risk," wrote Norges Bank Investment Management in September 2023 when it released its updated expectations on climate risk. The group manages Norway's $1.4 trillion sovereign wealth fund, the largest such fund in the world. Also known as "The Oil Fund," the group invests surplus profits from Norway's giant oil and gas reserves.[5]

Like Engine No. 1, Norges hasn't been shy about removing board members from its portfolio holdings over the importance of the climate issue.[6] Yet even Norges seems to backpedal, and reportedly the trust has once again increased its stakes in fossil fuels.[7] It's the two steps forward, one step back progress so common with climate issues.

Australia Retirement Trust is another money manager that has embraced environmental, sustainable, and governance (ESG) investing. "Effective stewardship of the retirement savings of members" requires the fund to integrate ESG considerations at all levels, the trust states on its website. "Managing risks emanating from ESG factors is consistent with pursuing the best financial interests of members."[8]

Given the polarization of the ESG moniker today, regardless of how it's referred to in the future, it's certainly not going away and likely will expand in scope to encompass more financial risk factors.

Stressed Markets

Beyond the debate over the more esoteric ramifications of socially responsible investing, climate change creates unpredictable risks and vulnerabilities financially and physically. That's because climate-related events can disrupt the supply and demand mechanisms of capitalism.

And when supply chains are interrupted and supplies tighten, prices climb, scarcity increases, and markets stress. All that leads to higher prices.

Dramatic Weather Events

Dramatic weather events like hurricanes and typhoons, destructive windstorms, massive rain events, flooding, and drought can lead to out-of-control wildfires, make roads impassable, ground airplanes, damage production facilities, and severely hamper agriculture production. For every 1°C increase in Earth's atmospheric temperature, water vapor in the air can increase 7%, according to the laws of thermodynamics.[9] All of that stresses supplies and markets. Even slowly rising sea levels can be problematic, generate unnecessary expenses, and force repricing to account for the added expenses.

Alternative sources of energy like wind and solar can suffer adverse impacts associated with massive meteorological events. That in turn hampers their ability to generate energy and disrupts supplies to markets.

As global warming continues and sea levels rise, huge chunks of island nations will become uninhabitable or disappear. That's not conjecture; that's a fact, and it is expected to happen this century. The Maldives, Tuvalu, the Marshall Islands, Nauru, and Kiribati are in "extreme danger," according to the UN Intergovernmental Panel on Climate Change. Kiribati only has an average elevation of about six feet above sea level.[10]

Out-of-Control Fires

Wildfires fueled by drought and global warming already have cost cities, towns, communities, governments, and businesses dearly. Those costs continue to add up around the globe.

California wineries alone lost approximately $3.7 billion following wildfires in 2020. Wineries in France, Greece, Italy, Portugal, Spain, Argentina, and Australia also have dealt with devastating wildfires and their economic fallout. Beyond the physical destruction of buildings and vines, wildfire smoke and ash that rains down on vineyards contains a chemical called *guaiacol* that can change a grape's flavor profile and leave an unpleasant aftertaste. Entire stocks of a particular vintage or even from a vineyard have had to be tossed out.[11]

Humans aren't the only ones affected by these wildfires. Livestock animals also suffer. Beef producers reported livestock losses due to burns and burn-associated deaths or euthanasia, according to a survey evaluating the impacts of the 2020 wildfire season on beef cattle, dairy cattle, sheep, and goat producers in California, Oregon, and Nevada. Dairy, beef, sheep, and goat producers also saw reduced conception, poor weight gain, and drops in milk production. All but dairy producers also saw pneumonia in their livestock. Lower birth weights, increased abortion rates, and unexplained deaths were reported in beef cattle, sheep, and goats. That doesn't factor in pasture destruction or other related property loss.[12]

All of this happened several years ago and only in the western United States. There have been and continue to be many more recent, dramatic, and intense wildfires around the globe that cause great destruction and greater carbon releases that hamper the quest for net zero.

For those who doubt the power of these climate-fueled fiascos, talk to survivors of the 2023 conflagration that wiped away moisture-parched Lahaina on Maui in Hawaii, or former residents of Fort Myers Beach, Florida, still struggling in September 2023, a year after Hurricane Ian ripped across its shores, wiping away huge swaths of that once-booming beach town. Or, listen to President Anote Tong of the Oceania nation of Kiribati talk to the UN General Assembly about rising sea levels that threaten his nation.[13]

Employee Risk

"Climate risk will become employee experience risk," Forrester warns in its "Predictions 2024." The global market researchers point to sizzling heat waves that led to labor strikes and contract negotiations around the globe in 2023.[14]

Whatever the industry, for people who work outside or in non-climate-controlled environments, rising temperatures as well as bone-chilling cold as a result of our climate changing make a difference, and one that hits businesses at the bottom line. Forrester goes on to predict, "non-union workers will use organized labor's blueprint, employing legal precedent established by a Montana state court and leaning on U.S. OSHA protections to assure safe and healthful working conditions in order to force their companies into policy changes and investments to adapt to the ongoing effects of climate change."[15]

Financial Regulators

All these tales of destruction and market disruption in mind should be a wake-up call for investors and consumers. The money we spend and invest can either contribute to improving society and our way of life or maintain the status quo, a planet with its climate in extreme peril.

Regulators are worried and corporations should be, too, because it's what we don't know that creates the potential for even greater risk. Risk and mitigation of climate change should figure into planning and strategies, period.

Climate risks could, for example, exacerbate financial system vulnerabilities that have little to do with climate change, like historically high levels of corporate leverage, according to the US Commodity Futures Trading Commission Report of the Climate-Related Market Risk Subcommittee, Market Risk Advisory Committee.[16]

Fiduciary Responsibilities

When consumers want more of something, suppliers usually produce or acquire more supplies to meet demand. With the case of climate, there still is resistance to sustainable investing even though public sentiment and stakeholders have pushed companies to pay attention.

Until recently, boards of directors, investor groups, and others often blamed their inaction or limited action on climate issues on their preference for short-term profits over ESG goals. But as more experts—legal scholars, governments, the United Nations, and beyond—see ESG investing as crucial to the future of our planet, investment approaches have changed direction. The latest consensus is that investment advisers, financial and accounting specialists, and fund and money managers as well as corporations have a legal, moral, and *fiduciary* duty to consider climate shifts in their financial decisions.

WTW (formerly known as Willis Towers Watson) is clear on the importance of this different approach. "Climate change [is] no longer a moral issue, but a fiduciary duty for boards," the company wrote in a recent Pay Memo for North America. "Directors should ask themselves which presents the greater risk—that they might draw censure for taking actions that compromise the company's near-term profitability or face personal liability if they fall short of addressing climate risks (including the physical, transition, and liability risks) and ensuring long-term sustainability of company."[17]

Courts in the United States have entered the fray, as activists take on the fossil fuel industry via lawsuits that address climate shifts.

In mid-2023, a group of young environmentalists in Montana won their case in state court, claiming state lawmakers violated their constitutional rights in ignoring the planet-warming effects of fossil fuel projects. That ruling is under appeal, but other similar cases have been filed in other states. Of note, also in 2023, the US Supreme Court rejected requests by big oil to rule on whether climate liability lawsuits belong in federal court.[18]

Whatever the final outcome of these court cases, it's clear climate risk and accountability isn't going away and increasingly will play a bigger role in decision-making in the future.

Market Demands Lead to Innovations

To foment periods of great innovation, multiple market forces must converge—cultural, geopolitical, supply, and demand. With capitalism behind it, there's no limit to what we can achieve moving forward.

New Possibilities

Technological innovation and growth are at the forefront. On the one hand, growth creates demand for more energy that produces more greenhouse gas (GHG) emissions and exacerbates the climate crisis. On the other hand, capitalism-fueled technological innovation also opens the doors to the possibility to discover more and better approaches to sustainability, new types of alternative energy production, new and better options to lithium-ion batteries for energy storage, creation of new biodegradable materials in place of ones that aren't, new approaches to measuring carbon emissions, and so much more.

While at Chesapeake Energy, I first saw how unreliable and rudimentary most forms of carbon accounting were. Most of this work was done in spreadsheets and reliability of data was limited.

There was no set of enterprise-grade software products that could reliably track, measure, quantify, and report the company's accurate and ongoing carbon footprint; knowing that information is crucial to facilitating organization-wide strategies to minimize GHG emissions and meet our neutrality goals.

We launched Persefoni, a software-as-service (SaaS) company to develop and market what I saw as a viable, accurate software solution to the carbon accounting dilemma. Even better, the software could provide continual updates to the ever-changing rules and regulations governing GHG emissions and environmental sustainability. Standardized measurements and protocols could be embedded into the platform for greater transparency and assurance. That's as opposed to the traditional black box approach that many legacy providers offer customers.

Today there are several SaaS options to help companies with their carbon accounting, and we're proud to have played a pivotal role in helping grow this niche industry to much broader global recognition.

In Pursuit of New Solutions to GHG Emissions

Another climate-related challenge that led to an innovative solution is the use of sulfur hexafluoride (SF_6), the most potent GHG known currently. Electric utilities rely on the synthetic fluorinated compound for voltage electrical insulation, current interruption, and arc quenching.

This climate-destroying gas is 23,500 times more effective at trapping infrared radiation than an equivalent amount of CO_2 and has an atmospheric lifetime of 3,200 years. As a result, a relatively small amount of SF_6 can significantly and negatively affect global climates.[19]

Because of its potency, consumers—including utilities employees who worked with SF_6—demanded an alternative. So, GE Grid Solutions, in partnership with 3M™ Company, developed a viable, available, and more environmentally friendly alternative known as g^3 (pronounced g cubed). g^3 products have "more than 99% less gas global warming potential (GWP)," comparatively, according to GE.[20]

GE also is involved in another environmentally friendly innovation in the energy space, Nant de Drance, which is a pumped storage hydropower plant in the Swiss Alps that provides energy storage without the negative environmental effects of lithium-ion batteries. The plant's reversible turbines can store energy or provide it with the flip of a switch.[21]

Sustainable aviation fuel (SAF) is yet another promising innovation with the potential to stem global GHG emissions up to 80%, according to the International Air Transport Association.[22] Aviation globally accounts for 2% of human-caused GHG emissions and 12% of all transportation emissions. The alternative fuel is made from renewable nonpetroleum feedstocks, including oil, fats, and waste. SAFs, depending on how they're produced, can be used alone or blended with other fuels.

Airline use of 100% SAF has the potential to reduce GHG emissions by up to 94%. Already more than 360,000 commercial flights, primarily in the United States and Europe, have relied at least partly on SAFs.[23] Demand for SAF is high as airlines scramble to find a solution to their fossil fuel consumption.

A Gulfstream G600 flew the first-ever 100% SAF-powered trans-Atlantic flight in November 2023. The first trans-Atlantic commercial flight powered by the same biofuel happened a little more than a week later when Virgin Atlantic Airlines flew a Boeing 787 Dreamliner nonstop from London to New York City.[24]

Currently, cost remains a roadblock with the commercial viability of widespread SAF use. The International Air Transport Association estimates that during 2022, SAF cost about $2,400/ton, about two-and-one-half times greater than the price of conventional jet fuel. Those prices could drop, however, with market competition, increased production, and expanding the feedstock mix used for production.[25]

"Flight100 (as Virgin named its flight) proves that Sustainable Aviation Fuel can be used as a safe, drop-in replacement for fossil-derived jet fuel and it's the only viable solution for decarbonizing long haul aviation," Virgin CEO Shai Weiss said following the flight. "It's taken radical collaboration to get here and we're proud to have reached this important milestone, but we need to push further. There is simply not enough SAF and it's clear that in order to reach production at scale, we need to see significantly more investment. This will only happen when regulatory certainty and price support mechanisms, backed by government, are in place."[26]

These are just several of the many ongoing innovations that have the potential of a positive effect on our climate. Some remain seeds of an idea, while others are in development, in use, or already making a difference.

As Virgin Atlantic CEO Shai so aptly pointed out, to move forward with these new innovations to combat the climate crisis requires the right kind of governance in terms of financial investments and support, as well as more innovations, along with widespread acceptance and use of standards to achieve our goals and eventually reach net zero.

The Value of Information

For innovations to occur, though, they also must begin with the right information. Often overlooked or ignored, information that is accurate and clear is crucial to successfully navigate and conquer climate challenges. Different parties with differing ideas and viewpoints must be willing to share accurate, robust, and thorough information without the private agendas that have been so common in the past.

Transparency and Clarity

Corporations need clear and updated reports on the financial risks associated with climate change. We're talking about accurate facts and figures, and strategies to achieve specific goals. Boards of directors must be upfront with stakeholders on whether sustainability is part of a company's vision and how it's being achieved.

I don't believe companies are inherently good or bad, and I do recognize that there are multiple sides and outcomes for every challenge and every solution. That said, companies and stakeholders must be open and willing to understand the broad ramifications of actions and reactions.

Global carbon accounting standards are in existence or in development, but they're not applied evenly or accurately, and even if they were, these standards alone aren't enough. Even with audit firms and assurances, numbers can be misconstrued and things get overlooked. Stakeholders, governments, regulators, investors, and concerned individuals need access to clear, concise, and accurate information. When we have that transparency, we can better understand the extent of the challenges and work successfully to find the solutions.

Markets function best when supported by a foundation of clear rules and accurate information. Simply relying on the market forces without addressing these crucial elements can hinder their ability to effectively solve problems like carbon emissions reductions.

Accurate Weather Data

It's no surprise that supply chains also need accurate weather data for long-term as well as short-term planning and risk assessment. For those who think linking accurate weather data and climate challenges is a bit far-fetched, consider that the socioeconomic benefits of weather prediction equate to at least $160 billion a year. Improving that forecasting and early warning of what's to come could add another $30 billion to that number, according to the UN World Meteorological Organization.[27]

Changing climate currently doesn't affect the accuracy of weather forecasting near term. That's because weather forecasts today rely in part on atmospheric physics as opposed to the historical datasets of years ago. Nonetheless climate issues still can affect supply chains. Unexpected severe weather, for example, can wipe out and/or shrink product supplies. Consider the effect of out-of-control wildfires on vineyards, livestock, or crops as mentioned previously.

Some experts also say that a warming climate might make it more difficult to predict hurricane intensity, and therefore preparedness. However, winter storms could move more slowly and become more predictable, according to Kerry Emanuel, professor emeritus of atmospheric science at Massachusetts Institute of Technology.[28]

A warming planet also can make long-range accurate weather predictions more difficult, especially for Earth's midlatitudes, says atmospheric scientist Aditi Sheshadri, lead author of a 2021 study by Stanford University. "Cooler climates seem to be inherently more predictable."

Sheshadri's research "suggests the window for accurate forecasts in the midlatitudes is several hours shorter with every degree (Celsius) of warming. This could translate to less time to prepare and mobilize for big storms in balmy winters than in frigid ones."[29]

A Circular Economy on the Horizon?

Beyond the weather effects, supply and demand require us to rethink how businesses operate. As leaders, we need to anticipate a changing buyer demographic now more than ever focused on sustainability and purpose.

One nascent economic approach gaining momentum from businesses, including some energy companies, is the idea of embracing a circular economy. That's as opposed to the more traditional linear approach—take, make, dispose—which has dominated our capitalism and fueled climate problems for so long. Contrast that to a circular economy that's all about reduce, recycle, and reuse.

A circular economy aims to break the link between economic growth and resource consumption. This is achieved through a closed-loop system where waste is minimized, and materials and energy are reused.

Circularity is centered on three principles:

- Use renewable inputs.
- Extend the lifespan of the product.
- Recover materials from by-products and waste.

Companies in the energy, utilities, and resources sector have the potential to play a huge role in the development of a circular economy.

Hoover CS is one of those companies working with a circular economy in mind. The Texas-based company provides sustainable packaging systems to the petroleum, refining, gas processing, and petrochemical manufacturing industries. To help companies move away from single-use containers, Hoover offers rental fleets of reusable intermediate bulk containers, bins, and special tanks.[30]

Further optimizing a company's environmental footprint, Hoover uses water reclamation systems to recycle water needed to clean its containers. With reduced plastic use, water conservation, and lower GHG emissions, it's a win, win, win for everyone.

Conflicting or Commendable?

The road to solutions is long and winding, controversial at times, and commendable. Riverstone Holdings LLC is a major global energy and power-focused private equity firm touted for its commitment to sustainability, accountability, and strict ESG goals. It also provides a good example of how the energy sector's knowledge and innovation can contribute to solving the climate challenges one step at a time.

In February 2023, Riverstone was part of a group of major investors in Michigan-based ONE, Our Next Energy Inc., an energy storage technology company focused on engineering batteries that will accelerate electrification. The company plans to open its first LFP (lithium-iron-phosphate) cell factory in 2024.[31]

LFP rechargeable batteries are considered more environmentally friendly than the currently more common lithium-ion batteries used in electric vehicles as well as power storage for renewables. Their demand also is expected to skyrocket in the coming years.[32]

In the last few years Riverstone has invested billions of dollars into coal-fired power plants through its Onyx Power Group in Europe with plans to transform them into high-efficiency and lower carbon-emitting plants. Onyx also says it's committed "if possible," to convert its existing coal-fired power plants to alternative and CO_2-neutral fuels by 2030. In another sustainability twist, Riverstone, through Onyx, has announced plans to build a blue hydrogen plant in proximity to one of its coal-fired plants near the port of Rotterdam, the Netherlands. According to Onyx, the new plant set to come online in 2028, could produce approximately 300 kilotons per year of low-CO_2 blue hydrogen, and save 2.5 million tons of CO_2 per year by using CO_2 capture and storage in nearby existing depleted gas fields.[33]

Time will tell if these ideas and innovations that sound or seem environmentally positive can come to fruition, scale, and make a difference toward our climate.

The Big Picture: A Chapter Roundup

- Climate risk is financial risk because it creates unpredictable financial and physical vulnerabilities that can disrupt the supply and demand mechanisms of capitalism.
- On the macro and micro levels, consumers, businesses, and governments want action to combat the climate crisis. Boardrooms, governments, and investor groups have listened and are taking action.
- Global GHG emissions accounting standards are in place, but they require improved rigor and consistency for more uniform application of the existing standards.

- Stakeholders, governments, regulators, and concerned individuals need access to clear, concise, and accurate information, including financial and physical risks related to the climate crisis.
- Creating a circular economy based on reduce, recycle, and reuse is an approach that is gaining momentum. That's compared with the more traditional linear approach—take, make, dispose.

PART

II

How Capitalism Will Solve the Climate Crisis

6

The Principles of Stakeholder Capitalism

"Money is a tool; energy is a resource."

I FIRMLY BELIEVE capitalism is the construct that will create the next wave of innovations that enable us to not just make it through the climate crisis but also to come out of it better.

Capitalism, consumerism, and the same market forces that caused the problem provide the environment for the necessary solutions. Those solutions come in the form of companies, products, new technologies, and new businesses and financial models.

The Power of Innovation

This *will* happen because periods of profound innovation always occur during times of great need or technological advancements—hence the popular saying, "necessity is the mother of invention." Think about innovations and discoveries like Jonas Salk's polio vaccine, which was discovered amid a polio epidemic, the revolutionary mRNA COVID-19 vaccine developed during the recent pandemic, and the internet, which came about during the Cold War initially as a tool for the US military to share information securely.

I believe this energy transition or climate tech boom has already begun and the new stakeholder capitalism will thrive moving forward based on broad metrics that include environmental and social impacts. Whatever the moniker or the timing, underlying the boom is the global transition from an economy that consumes fossil fuels indiscriminately to one that seeks out cleaner energies and counts our planet's climate as a stakeholder.

Great Economic Value

This energy transition and decarbonization effort will unlock economic value and tremendous wealth creation as people and companies seize this great opportunity. The CO_2 removal industry alone could be worth up to $1.2 trillion to remove gigatons of carbon from the atmosphere by 2050, according to market projections. And that's just the economic potential of one industry.

Companies positioned to address the challenges of decarbonization stand to gain significant advantages, which include the following:

- Enhance efficiencies and cost-effectiveness across operations, potentially creating new markets for low-carbon solutions.
- Strategize on low emission products and processes to replace existing high-carbon ones—electric vehicles (EVs), for example, which replace internal combustion vehicles.
- Create new initiatives to support the production of low carbon products and processes in the first two categories.

A Convergence

Although the opportunities for business and profit creation in the sector are a critical ingredient, opportunity alone is never enough to fuel the necessary advances for great economic and technological leaps forward. As history has shown during other times of great innovation and change, multiple market forces, including cultural, geopolitical, and other drivers, also must come to a head simultaneously.

The origins of this stakeholder capitalism can be traced to the 1960s and 1970s when growing numbers of businesses and leaders began to recognize that their actions affected more than only their shareholders. Largely that was a result of the environmental impacts from industrial sectors that led to dramatic changes to the Clean Water Act and the passage of the Clean Air Act.

Externalities at the time provided a visible picture of the negative environmental impacts. The Cuyahoga River fire of 1969 in Cleveland, Ohio, is the poster child example. Though the heavily industrial-polluted river had caught fire a number of times previously, this brief—20-minute—fire caused by an oil slick in the middle of the choked river became the symbol of the need to pay attention to the environmental impacts of capitalism.[1] The fire delivered the message that companies and their executives had a responsibility to consider the interests of all their stakeholders—not just their shareholders—when making decisions.

Long-Term Value Creation

Stakeholders have become power shifters, and their actions are a critical element to solve the climate crisis. Widespread anger and frustration, after all, often lead to system-level change, so much so that climate risk assessment and decision-making today can have dramatic bottom-line ramifications like long-term value creation or lack thereof.

In 2019, a coordinated climate action walkout was planned by tech employees across the nation, including at Google, Amazon, Microsoft, and others. The protestors urged the industry and world leaders to increase efforts in climate change. In a move seen by some as a response to employee concerns, Amazon launched a groundbreaking plan called The Climate Pledge, a commitment to net-zero emissions by 2040—10 years ahead of the 2050 Paris Agreement.[2]

The Amazon scenario is not isolated. Increasingly it's happening around the globe among not only companies and industries but also governments and private organizations. For many in the developed world, the practice of analyzing externalities once thought extemporaneous now has become important to a business's reputation, ability to operate, and its long-term viability.

Even in lower socioeconomic portions of the world, people and stakeholders alike are waking up to negative environmental externalities and choosing to protect the environment over solely the profit motive. In late November 2023, for example, the Supreme Court of

Panama ruled against Canadian mining giant First Quantum Minerals, forcing the closure of its Cobre Panama in Donoso, one of the world's largest open-pit copper mines. That move left more than 4,000 people out of work. The ruling and the closing came following massive public protests over fears the mine was harming the environment, including the area's water supply.[3]

The tobacco industry in the United States is another example of stakeholders taking action. As consumers became more aware of the impacts of tobacco on their health, many began to change their habits and quit smoking. Similarly, as consumers become more aware of the impacts of certain products or activities on our climate, many have begun to change their behaviors, demand more sustainable products, and more sustainably responsible actions from companies, organizations, and governments.

On a smaller scale, remember SF_6, the extremely potent greenhouse gas (GHG) I mentioned in Chapter 5? Stakeholders recognized the dangers of working with and the environmental impacts of SF_6 so they stepped up and demanded an alternative. GE Grid Solutions, in partnership with 3M™ Company, developed g^3 as an alternative.

The Role of Entrepreneurs

We're now at a point in time where entrepreneurs are more celebrated than ever before. Couple that with the rise of social entrepreneurship—creating a business that aims to generate positive social and environmental impact—and it's easily apparent why we're about to witness a great period of climate- and energy-related innovation.

Evolving Landscape

Since the dot-com boom in the late 1990s, the venture capital industry has played a key role in the radical advancement of countless industries. Along the way, stories of generational wealth-creation opportunities quickly advanced from concept to reality. The stories of entrepreneurship and the most well-known mega successes to come out of Silicon Valley deeply changed the calculus of how wealth could be created and sought.

For decades prior to the dot-com boom, Wall Street had been the predominant destination for those looking to take maximum advantage of the profit opportunities capitalism had to offer. Then Silicon Valley entrepreneurs and investors began to prove a new model, and Wall Street quickly had competition. This rise of Silicon Valley and entrepreneurship have had profound impacts on the global economy. Crucial is that the unique Silicon Valley startup ecosystem "grew out of a specific regional context at a particular historical moment and developed hand-in-hand with particular technological opportunities and organizational experimentations," writes Kenji Kushida, in an article for the Carnegie Endowment for International Peace.[4]

Along the way, entrepreneurship and creating the next big thing became for many as much about social currency and status as it did financial returns. As of 2023, there were 594 million entrepreneurs in the world, up 2.1% from the 582 million in 2020.[5]

Powering this growth of entrepreneurs has been the democratization of information and other technological innovations like the internet and the cloud that provide current and prospective entrepreneurs significantly lower barriers to getting started.

As important, in recent decades, startups have had more opportunities to access the capital they need to grow. Since the early 2010s alone, the venture capital industry has matured significantly, and is among the highest performing asset classes. This track record of performance has naturally attracted even more capital into the industry, resulting in more firms and more capital to invest.

Making a Difference

When we overlay these developments with the more recent rise of social entrepreneurism and impact investing, we begin to see economic and cultural market forces starting to align for the perfect period of climate positive innovation incubation.

Social entrepreneurs, those who identify a social problem and develop a business model to address it, are driven by a desire to create positive change in the world. They work across many fields, from environmental sustainability to health care and education.

Like traditional entrepreneurs, social entrepreneurs seek to create value for their stakeholders. However, they focus on scaling businesses and solutions that have a positive impact on society or the environment in conjunction with profits, rather than in lieu of them.

That distinction is critical because no matter how important social or environmental causes are to investors, the overwhelming majority aren't willing to forgo any level of reduced return potential in exchange for positive nonfinancial impact.

Though greed always plays a role, this largely stems from the legal constructs of market-based economies that dictate shareholder value is defined financially. As such, companies and their executives, especially those in publicly traded companies, often have been legally bound to prioritize the financial well-being of their stakeholders.

But, as I mentioned in Part I of this book, that's begun to change as legal and investment experts begin to call for corporate and investment risk assessments that take into account climate change and point to the fiduciary duty that goes with it.

Profits and More

It's not just entrepreneurs who face the challenge of satisfying shareholders. Unilever, the United Kingdom–based global consumer products company, is a prime example of the planning, performance, visions, and conflicts that plague many typical efforts to curb climate shifts, encourage sustainability, and lead to clashes with shareholders.

A long-time leader in sustainable sourcing, responsible water use, and green farming initiatives, Unilever pledged to have zero carbon emissions from its own products and to halve the GHG footprint of its products by 2030. The company also set a goal of net-zero emissions from all its products by 2039.[6]

Those are admirable goals and certainly for any company, of any size, worth emulating. However, as with the sustainability goals of so many other companies, implementation at Unilever has fallen short. Shareholders aren't happy either. Indicative of the chasm that divides leaders in the business world, those investors rail at relinquishing profits in favor of planet sustainability goals.

Concerns have been raised regarding a potential imbalance within the company, where the emphasis on public sustainability image might be overshadowing core business priorities. As of September 2023, Unilever had replaced sustainability advocate and then-CEO Alan Jope, who wasn't on track with achieving its emissions and financial goals.[7]

Impact Investing

Corresponding to the rise of social entrepreneurship has been that of impact investing. Though similar to environmental, social, and governance (ESG) investing, the two are not the same. Impact investing aims to generate both financial return and social or environmental impact, and it involves investing in companies, organizations, and funds that are working to solve social or environmental challenges and create a positive impact on society or the environment. However, ESG investing, as mentioned previously, focuses on identifying companies based on their ESG practices. For example, ESG investing might involve a stock index that excludes companies with poor environmental records and health and safety practices.

Like social entrepreneurship, impact investments can be made in a variety of sectors, including clean energy, affordable housing, education, and health care, among others.

Unlike traditional philanthropy, which involves donating money to a cause, impact investing involves the deployment of capital with the expectation of financial return and measurable social or environmental impact.

Impact investments take many forms, including direct investments in impact-focused companies or organizations, investments in funds that focus on impact investing, and investments in traditional assets with a focus on ESG criteria. Impact investors might also use their platform and influence to advocate for policy and regulatory change that supports the achievement of their social and environmental goals.

The Link to Solving the Climate Crisis

All these different market forces, business models, and profit opportunities create a powerful precedent for innovation, especially in the context of the climate crisis. After all, crucial periods of innovation happened during times of great danger, crisis, or war. From a more philosophical viewpoint, the threat of annihilation or loss of a resource serves as a call to action.

The climate crisis will tip many parts of the world into great conflict, and as such it inadvertently creates pressure points that are important for innovation. Crises often create a sense of urgency, collaborations, and a need for immediate solutions, which can lead to the development of new ideas and technologies. When people are faced with a crisis, they might be more likely to take risks and think creatively to find a solution to the challenge. This can lead to the development of new technologies or approaches that might not have been considered otherwise. I mentioned a few previously in this chapter.

Technological advancements by their own merits, of course, will not solve the climate crisis. And there is no one silver bullet, either. Just as there are a wide array of market forces and factors that led to the creation of the climate crisis in the first place, there will be an equally wide array of these to solve them.

More specifically, nearly every capitalist market force and actor who played a role in creating the problem will play a role in its solution. The financial sector and governments are chief among them, but there is one that trumps them all. Consumerism will play a leading role in the solution.

Many already are demanding more sustainable products and services across nearly every part of the economy and voters will demand action from their governments to protect their health and well-being. This greening of the economy has begun and will only accelerate from here. Whether it is us buying sneakers made from recycled plastic bottles or governments creating financial incentives for auto manufacturers to produce EVs, the forces of capitalism are at work solving our global emissions problem.

Take Amazon again, for example. The company invested $2 billion through The Climate Pledge Fund to support the development of sustainable technologies and engaged over 400 companies to support their 2040 net-zero carbon commitment.[8]

Today some of the sustainability statistics Amazon highlights on its website include the following:

- 90% of the electricity consumed by the company is attributable to renewable energy sources.
- The company remains on a path to 100% renewable energy by 2025, five years ahead of schedule.
- Expanded use of zero-emission transportation like EV cargo vans, cargo e-bikes, and on-foot deliveries.

■ Use of innovative construction techniques and building materials for its fulfillment centers, data centers, offices, and retail locations are more sustainable.

Energy Transition

Further recognition that stakeholder capitalism is making a difference comes from the latest edition of Schroders's flagship Institutional Investor Study. "Energy transition," the study found, promises an opportunity for investors looking to private equities. Further, almost half of those institutional investors polled (43%) highlight having a positive impact on people and the planet as a top driver for sustainable investing.

About half of global investors also like infrastructure and renewables as areas to make the most of energy transition investment opportunities in the medium term. Innovation in the energy transition space, too, promises opportunity for investment gains.[9]

As I mentioned previously, some investor groups worry that ESG investing is at the expense of performance and profits. However, that's not necessarily the case. Research suggests a positive connection between ESG factors and financial performance. The analysis indicates the following:

■ **Long-term benefits.** Companies with strong ESG practices tend to see more pronounced improvement in financial performance over extended periods.

■ **Crisis resilience.** Investments in ESG offers greater protection against economic or social downturns.

■ **Sustainability as a driver.** Implementing sustainable practices within corporations lead to better financial performance due to improved risk management and increased innovation.

■ **Carbon focus and financial gain.** Studies suggest that actively managing toward a low carbon future contributes to positive financial performance.

Studies also suggest that ESG stock performances can vary significantly. Depending on specific stocks and time frames involved, the performance of these ESG stocks or indexes will most likely cause mixed results.

Read the Fine Print

Of note, all companies that claim to be ESG investments might not be. Some stock indexes with the ESG designation quietly are embracing oil and gas investments.[10]

That's in part why regulators are cracking down on the use of the ESG moniker. Regulations like the SEC's proposed amendments to its rules under the Securities Act of 1933 and Securities Exchange Act of 1934 would require companies to disclose certain climate-related information to ensure companies aren't cheating their investors by claiming they're practicing ESG when they're not.[11]

Also, some people, concerned about the environment and tired of being misled by greenwashing, are looking to move away from buying the traditional Standard and Poor's 500. Instead, they're either turning to affect responsible investing or seeking out better and more reliable ESG funds to integrate in their investment portfolios.

Accountability

Concurrent to the rise of stakeholder capitalism is the demand for accountability on the part of businesses. Investors, consumers, and other stakeholders today want more information on how companies operate and their impact on society and the environment. In the climate space, that's led to the development of various reporting standards, discussed in Chapter 3.

It's worth restating that two of those standards-setting groups include the Global Reporting Initiative (GRI) and the Sustainability Accounting Standards Board (SASB). Both provide guidelines for organizations to follow when disclosing information about their sustainability and broader ESG practices.

Global Accountability

The recent formation of the International Sustainability Standards Board (ISSB) at COP26 was another monumental step for the world of corporate disclosure. As a standard-setting board, the ISSB delivers a comprehensive global baseline of sustainability-related disclosure standards. It enables companies around the world to report their ESG data under a unified set of standards. For investors that means the ability to easily compare companies by their sustainability-related risks and opportunities and make better informed decisions.

Those stakeholder demands also led to tools and initiatives that promote corporate accountability. For example, the CDP, formerly the Carbon Disclosure Project, is a global nonprofit organization that works with companies to measure and disclose their environmental impacts. By providing companies a platform to report on their sustainability practices, the CDP helps create transparency and accountability.

A few more organizations that promote corporate accountability include the following:

- **GHG Protocol for Project Accounting.** Specifies international standards for corporate GHG accounting and reporting; put together by the World Business Council for Sustainable Development and World Resources Institute in cooperation with global businesses and governments (GHGprotocol.org)
- **GRI.** Global Reporting Initiative, an independent international organization that pioneered sustainability reporting (www .globalreporting.org)
- **IIRC.** International Integrated Reporting Council, formerly the International Integrated Reporting Committee, and now part of IFRS Foundation, a cross-section of corporate, investment, accounting, securities, regulatory, academic and standard-setting sectors (www.integratedreporting.org)
- **ISO.** International Organization for Standardization, an independent, nongovernmental international organization of national standards bodies (www.iso.org)
- **SASB.** Sustainability Accounting Standards Board, an independent board accountable for the due process, outcomes, and ratification of SASB standards; now part of the IFRS Foundation (sasb.org/)
- **IPCC.** Intergovernmental Panel on Climate Change, United Nations panel that assesses science related to climate change (www.ipcc.ch)

- **IASB.** International Accounting Standards Board, an independent standard-setting body within the IFRS Foundation (www .ifrs.org); responsible for the development and publication of IFRS Accounting Standards

And these aren't all of the organizations in just the climate-related reporting space.

Similarly, the Global Compact is a United Nations' initiative that encourages companies to align their operations and strategies with universal principles on human rights, labor, anti-corruption, and the environment.

From increasing public pressure and regulatory frameworks to the recognition that corporate accountability is good for business, it's clear there is a growing expectation that companies will be held accountable for their actions and their impact on society and the environment. Already more than 23,000 companies reported their environmental data to the Carbon Disclosure Project in 2023, globally representing $67 trillion (more than 66% of global market capitalization).[12]

The Cost of Decarbonizing

Accountability, though, isn't cheap; it never is, whether the price to be paid is personal, financial, or some other construct. The road to net zero is no different as industry analysts suggest that the cost to reach net zero by 2050 will be about $275 trillion in cumulative spending on physical assets, or approximately $9.2 trillion per year between 2021 and 2050.

That's a tremendous bill, but achievable. Estimates place the climate adaptation market alone at $2 trillion a year by 2026. And that's simply for the cost of changes related to what's happening to our climate. A few examples of how people are adapting include farmers planting more heat-resistant crops or cities building higher seawalls, retrofitting the electric grid to withstand extreme weather events, and even building more weather-resistant buildings.[13]

Tough Shift

People often say money makes the world go 'round. A more accurate statement is energy makes the world go 'round. Think about it.

Energy provides opportunities and creates independence. In the western world, without energy we wouldn't have all our comforts. Offer $1,000 to someone in a lower socioeconomic country and that's an opportunity for them to access energy to drill a well for potable water or buy a solar or wind generator to heat their homes and cook indoors.

If you think that sounds a bit far-fetched, read the headlines that scream "Climate Change" and talk about missed GHG emissions goals, conflicts, critical temperature increases, and everything else climate related. As I write this book, it's the run-up and follow-up to COP, in this case, COP28. As you read previously, that's the annual United Nations meeting of parties to discuss climate developments and concerns. Discussions are rife with fears, concerns, criticisms, and pessimism, especially since the COP28 talks were held in oil-rich Dubai in 2023 and helmed by an oil sheik.

Yet there's also optimism for some of the same reasons. The most important direct manifestation of stakeholder capitalism in the climate space has been the proliferation of net-zero commitments by not only businesses but governments and countries as well.

As US climate envoy John Kerry said after the formal COP28 final document was signed, "There is cause for optimism." Even though the document fell short of calling for the phase out of fossil fuels, its nearly 200 signatories agreed to the "transitioning away" from fossil fuels by 2050.[14]

UN Emissions Gap Report 2023

On the agenda at COP28 was discussion of the world's progress, or lack thereof, toward achieving the goals laid out in the Paris Agreement. As is typical, there are multiple reports from multiple groups that track where we are or are not.

Though the details in each report vary somewhat, many of the answers to the general questions are similar. Are we close to reaching our goals? No. Are we much better off today than yesterday? Absolutely! Are more companies paying attention to the financial ramifications of climate? Definitely. Are governments paying attention? Definitely. Do we have much more to do as companies, countries, and people? Very much so.

Much of the discussion at COP28 was aimed at the continued reduction of the use of fossil fuels without much talk about how to replace the energy they produce and the world needs. To solve the crisis requires a balanced approach that takes into consideration the energy needs of the world, the impacts of human consumption, and the cost of alternatives and solutions. The seemingly one-sided nature of the many discussions reported in the mainstream media might be good for attracting viewers, but they're not helpful to actually solve the problems.

The UN Emissions Gap Report finds that there has been progress since the Paris Agreement was signed in 2015. GHG emissions in 2030, based on policies in place, were projected to increase by 16% at the time of the agreement's adoption. Today, the projected increase is 3%. However, predicted 2030 GHG emissions still must fall by 28% for the Paris Agreement 2°C pathway and 42% for the 1.5°C pathway.[15]

Let's look at a few more of the takeaways from this latest UN Emissions Gap Report 2023:

- Nine countries have submitted new or updated NDCs (nationally determined contribution) since COP 27; the total as of September 2023 is 149 (the EU counts as one entity). NDCs now contain specific GHG reduction targets and many encompass a country's entire economy instead of only certain sectors.
- Ninety-seven parties, accounting for 81% of global GHG emissions, have adopted net-zero pledges, up from 88 last year.
- Immediate, accelerated, and relentless mitigation action is needed to bring about the deep annual emission cuts that are required from now to 2030 to narrow the emissions gap, even without accounting for excess emissions since 2020.
- If current policies are continued, global warming is estimated to be limited to 3°C. Delivering on all unconditional and conditional pledges by 2030 lowers this estimate to 2.5°C, with the additional fulfillment of all net-zero pledges bringing it to 2°C.[16]

Net Zero Stocktake 2023

Just as the UN report revealed, the Net Zero Stocktake report shows progress in some areas and not in others. Still there's optimism that goals can be met. Net Zero Tracker, which is responsible for the

Stocktake, is a nonprofit consortium of four organizations: Energy and Climate Intelligence Unit, Oxford Net Zero, Data-Driven EnviroLab, and NewClimate Institute

Here are some highlights from the 2023 Net Zero Stocktake report, the organization's third assessment:

- Growth in the number of national and subnational net-zero targets has slowed, but company net-zero, target-setting momentum continues.
- The number of large public companies with net-zero targets more than doubled in two years—from 417 to 929.
- National government net-zero targets underpinned by legislation or policy documents increased in 2½ years, from 7% to 75%.
- A significant share of subnational and corporate entities still lack emissions reduction targets.
- Collectively, signs are limited of improvement in the robustness of subnational and corporate net-zero targets and strategies.
- More entities are clarifying their intention to use carbon dioxide removals in their value chain.
- Despite net-zero pledges, no major producer countries or companies have committed to phasing out fossil fuels. (An agreement at COP28 does call for eliminating the use of coal.)
- Emerging voluntary net-zero standards have converged on principles, but still need more specificity for clarity to entities that want to set credible strategies.
- Of the over 4,000 entities Net Zero Stocktake currently tracks, at least 1,475 now have a net-zero target, up from 769 in December 2020.[17]

The Social Media Effect

Social media, as I talked about previously, is the ultimate in oversight, weeding out the winners and the losers, the bad actors, and the truth tellers, especially in the climate space. It can also serve as a visual representation of how climate change affects a community while promoting awareness to the broad population.

Social media platforms hand a megaphone and an eager audience to anyone who wants to hold others to account, for better or worse. It provides a place where someone can tell a story and show the impacts of a crisis on their community. With the effects of the Canadian wildfires of June 2023, for example, in the United States, tourists and locals alike in New York City strapped on masks and began chronicling the dystopian orange skies on social media.

Those unforgettable images show us the dire consequences of our actions or inactions to combat climate change. Shared stories like these will continue to remind us of our current trajectory beyond the 2°C temperature rise as stipulated by the Paris Agreement. Whether someone is recording the collapse of a melting glacier in the Arctic or flooding and destruction in Pakistan, the images serve as a warning to the broader world that we all have a stake in finding a better path forward for our planet's future.

Social media has fueled the rising discourse about the physical impacts of climate change and the various aspects of capitalism that led us there. As in great periods of change, a level of discontent fuels these conversations, cemented in the uncertainty of our planet's future.

The Wealth Gap

This proliferation of social media also has accelerated the widening wealth gap. That's the disparity between the rich and poor that contributes to the rise of stakeholder capitalism.

A 2022 report notes how the poorest half of the global population owns just 2% of the world's wealth, with the average adult owning just $3,140. That's in contrast to the top 10% owning 76% of the world's wealth.[18] Those numbers are important in the context of the climate crisis because global economic inequalities are intertwined with disparities in contributions to GHG emissions. The top 1% of the world's population accounts for 17% of global carbon emissions; the top 10% for 48% of emissions, and the bottom 50% of the population just 12% of carbon emissions. Looking at it another way, the world's poorest 4 billion people contribute the least to the climate crisis, yet they remain the most vulnerable to the impacts of climate change.[19]

As discontent grows over this income disparity and climate shifts, as I mentioned previously, system-level change can and does happen.

The Big Picture: A Chapter Roundup

- This new energy transition will unlock tremendous economic value and wealth creation as people and companies take advantage of the great opportunities that lie ahead in the climate space.
- People often say money makes the world go 'round. A more accurate statement is energy makes the world go 'round.
- The most important direct manifestation of stakeholder capitalism is the extensive commitments to net zero by companies and countries alike.
- The UN Emissions Gap Report finds that there has been progress since the Paris Agreement was signed in 2015. GHG emissions in 2030 were projected to increase by 16% at the time of the agreement's adoption. Today, the projected increase is 3%.[20]
- Sustainability has gone mainstream. Only 3% of S&P 500 companies didn't disclose information about their overall ESG board governance approach in 2022.[21]
- Social media, especially its platform for visual representation, provides the ultimate lens and the ultimate oversight for weeding out the winners and the losers, the bad actors, and the truth tellers, especially in the climate space.

7

The Role of Modern Finance, Wall Street, and Private Equity

"Venture capitalists tend to be willing to take on higher-risk, early stage innovators and companies."

CAPITAL IS THE lifeblood of all companies, and as discussed, institutional capital plays a pivotal role during periods of great technological and economic growth. Today's climate crisis is no different.

The world of finance contributes to climate solutions through the following ways:

- Deployment of capital to finance research and development of new climate technologies and businesses
- Limits on capital deployment into sectors and businesses with high emissions
- Investors and lenders requiring companies to make and meet climate commitments
- Development of innovative climate-specific financial vehicles

Capital Is Essential

The availability of capital to finance research and development of new climate technologies is critical. Climate tech refers to technology

97

designed to mitigate or adapt to the impacts of climate change including to reduce greenhouse gas (GHG) emissions.

Venture Capital

As a new and developing sector and to scale to commercial viability, climate tech requires long-term-oriented capital instead of the more short-term-oriented returns required through public stock markets and loans. Public markets play a role in the later-stage scaling of new companies and technologies.

Private capital markets tend to have more success enabling and accelerating scientific breakthroughs and the commercialization of technologies. Much of that can be attributed to the maturation and growth of the venture capital (VC) industry, arguably the most critical form of financing today for taking ideas to the next level.

That's in part because VC firms and individuals tend to have longer profitability time horizons than most other investors. As important, the success of their investment model depends heavily on breakout successes, which means venture capitalists usually take on higher risk profile investments, especially in the early stages of a market.

To get a better idea of the size of the VC pool in terms of dollars and cents, in 2022, globally the amount of capital raised from traditional capital raising markets totaled $541.8 billion. The VC segment made up about 89% of that.[1]

Partnerships

Business leaders in the world of finance already are partnering with other experts to find better solutions. One of those partnerships is between BlackRock, Inc., a leading provider of financial technology, and Singapore-based global investor Temasek. Together, in 2021 the two organizations launched Decarbonization Partners, a series of late-stage venture capital and early-growth private equity investment to accelerate global efforts to achieve a net-zero economy by 2050.

To meet ambitious net-zero targets, these formidable goals require innovative decarbonization technologies and solutions that need to be scaled. Capital is essential not only to the mission of sustainability but also offers an attractive investment opportunity created by the global shift toward achieving net zero.

And, as is typical with stakeholder capitalism today, one partnership with a great idea spreads to others. In November 2023, BBVA, the Spanish multinational financial services company based in Madrid and Bilbao, Spain, announced a $25 million investment in climate fund Decarbonization Partners Fund I.[2]

Government Guarantees

Major funding for climate tech research and development—Climate Tech 1.0—came in 2009 from then President Barack Obama's administration. The American Recovery and Reinvestment Act of 2009 called for allocating billions of dollars for clean energy and climate tech projects, including the Clean Power Plan to reduce carbon emissions from power plants. The Paris Agreement also committed the United States and other nations to reduce GHG emissions.

Pros and Cons

However, these supportive policies, funding, and a greater public awareness of the climate crisis weren't enough to prevent the ultimate collapse of parts of this pro-climate wave. The final blow to the Clean Power Plan came in 2019 when the Trump administration's Environmental Protection Agency repealed the law.[3]

President Obama took all kinds of heat for the failure of various tech projects that received federal loan guarantees during his administration. The biggest and the most publicized failure was Solyndra, a manufacturer of advanced solar panels that received a $535 million loan guarantee.[4] In reality, the Energy Department's loan guarantee program that included Solyndra was created as part of the Energy Policy Act of 2005.[5]

In actual numbers, only 8% of companies that received loans from the Obama program went bankrupt, according to US Department of Energy numbers.[6] However, according to a 2016 study from the Massachusetts Institute of Technology Energy Initiative, venture capitalists spent more than $25 billion on clean energy technology from 2006 to 2011 and lost more than half their money.[7]

What drove those failures? Unrealistic expectations that commercial enterprises would step forward and embrace carbon accounting as the natural first step toward measuring their carbon footprint and then planning decarbonization strategies. Without investor or regulatory pressure at the time, executives were not interested in their carbon footprint, let alone having a third-party audit. In fact, not only were executives disinterested but also they preferred that the climate tech industry itself disappear to stop the inevitable questions about why they weren't moving forward.

Contributing to the collapse also were overly optimistic estimates for commercial viability of many of the big-ticket climate tech products. Although many of the endeavors showed promise, some were prohibitively expensive or impractical for widespread adoption.

Another reason the climate tech wave of the late 2000s never materialized is that ultimately long-term funding came up short. Despite the billions of dollars invested during this time, companies lacked the ongoing financial support to continue when markets failed to materialize in line with expectations.

The Standards Issue

As important as all the other issues in the wavering of Climate Tech 1.0 at the time was the lack of reasonable GHG emissions standards and reporting. While the Greenhouse Gas Protocol was in place, so too were dozens of other standards with few organizations actually using them. There was no consolidation into a single standard. As you read in Chapter 6, that's happening today with the International Sustainability Standards Board and its first two sets of standards, IFRS S1 and IFRS S2.

Adding to the problems with the first climate tech wave, without clear standards in place, it was cumbersome for new vendors to demonstrate the effectiveness of their products and for potential customers to compare products. Fossil fuels added stiff competition when it came to developing markets for climate tech products. In the first decade of the 2000s, fossil fuels remained the low-cost dominant power source.

The Rise of Climate Tech 2.0

Though some segments quickly labeled Obama's climate initiatives a failure, reality is that they helped lay the groundwork for Climate Tech 2.0, the newest wave of climate technology innovations and changes. Climate Tech 2.0 includes a vast array of technologies related to climate change, from mitigation and adaptation to energy, agriculture, transportation, construction, manufacturing, and retail.

Despite efforts to quash climate initiatives after the Obama administration, more stakeholders and organizations began to talk seriously about widespread standards for GHG emissions. Capital investments in climate technologies increased dramatically—from $8 billion in 2017 to $37 billion in 2021.[8] States, organizations, and companies launched new green initiatives and developed new innovations.

Reasons for the rise of Climate Tech 2.0 include broader acceptance of climate change, greater public and private climate pledges to net zero, more policy and regulatory support, climate technology needs by corporations to achieve climate commitments and transition their businesses, and improved maturation and commercial viability of technologies involved.[9]

Throughout this book, I talk about many of those companies and initiatives either born from or stimulated by this new wave of climate technologies. Even those initiatives launched prior to Climate Tech 2.0 gained new traction and more support, whether financially or otherwise from stakeholders and innovators.

Both public and private entities learned well from the lessons of Climate Tech 1.0 and are moving forward with new and better approaches that address the issues of economics, scale, widespread acceptance, and viable business models.

The Big Picture: A Chapter Roundup

- Capital—both public and private—to finance research and development of new climate technologies is critical.
- Private capital markets tend to have more success enabling and accelerating scientific breakthroughs and the commercialization of technologies because they are less encumbered by short-term profit demands.

- Among the reasons the Obama era climate tech push didn't materialize to the extent expected were continued doubts about climate change, the lack of ongoing financing, and absent broadly accepted clear standards.
- Climate Tech 2.0 took off because climate change culture mattered, along with increasing regulatory standards and financial support.

8

Governance, Promoting Capitalism, and Efficient Free Market Economies

"History has proven that during great crises governments can mobilize forces, public and private, to meet the greatest challenges."

UNTIL RELATIVELY RECENTLY, long-term shifts in our climate have been a nonfactor in the quantum of government decision-making. Policies and legislation instead overwhelmingly focused on achieving economic growth and prosperity with capitalism as the basis of economic practices. It left consumerism and corporations to largely dictate humanity's future.

But today's rapidly heating climate and the destructive nature of extreme weather demands strong climate governance now. Voluntary or mired-in-politics compliance is no longer enough to overcome the worsening effects of growing greenhouse gas (GHG) emissions on the availability of natural resources and the long-term viability of our environment as we know it.

Typically, governments move slowly to develop policies, rules, regulations, tariffs, and incentives or to foster public and private partnerships, especially when they relate to our environment. Enforcement efforts often end up too little or too late to make enough difference.

As the World Bank (and so many others) so aptly points out, "strong governance systems are central" to helping countries reach their climate goals and curtail rising global temperatures.[1]

Fortunately, as I said previously in this book, during times of great crisis, history has proven that governments can mobilize the economic forces required to meet their constituencies' greatest challenges, whether economic or physical. In this case, the crisis to be managed is both and affects all of us.

Strong and Definitive Policies

Supportive governance can encourage innovation and compliance. Right and fair policies can make or break new and different approaches. Conversely, the wrong incentives or lax governance can exacerbate the problems.

Governments look to subsidies in whatever form—whether tax breaks, cash or grants, special financing terms like the loan guarantees from the Obama administration mentioned in Chapter 7, or some other favorable agreement—to achieve strategic objectives that are economic, political, geopolitical, and environmental. Incentives could include taxes or tariffs that create barriers to and limit the use of non-renewable materials or bolster production of more environmentally friendly alternatives.

In December 2022, for example, the US Department of Energy announced $3.7 billion in incentives to kickstart GHG removal.[2] Then in November 2023, with the goal of strengthening the supply chain, the US Department of Energy announced up to $3.5 billion in incentives for companies that produce lithium-ion batteries and the minerals that go into them. These batteries currently play a dominant role in EVs and are critical to energy storage powered by renewable energy sources like wind and solar.[3]

Stark Climate Reality

As the Obama-era Climate Tech 1.0 collapse shows, not enough as well as the wrong types of incentives, lack of ongoing support, and politics can have disastrous results on a nascent economic sector like climate tech.

Let's look at fossil fuel incentives. Globally, subsidies totaled $7 trillion in 2022 or 7.1% of GDP. Almost 60% of those subsidies were the result of undercharging for global warming and local air pollution, according to the International Monetary Fund.[4]

Once again, these numbers indicate the importance of taking the right actions in the right time frame, and how that can make a tremendous difference in the fight to reclaim our climate security.

Standard Protocols

Unquestionably broad standardization of protocols and reporting also is crucial to solving our climate challenges. That's a primary reason the GHG Protocol for Project Accounting (GHGprotocol.org) was developed. It specifies international standards for corporate GHG accounting and reporting and was put together by the World Business Council for Sustainable Development and World Resources Institute in cooperation with global businesses and governments. The idea was to create a global standard for accounting and reporting much like the Generally Accepted Accounting Principles and International Accounting Standards from the International Accounting Standards Board.

But just because standards are in place doesn't mean they are accepted, adhered to, and applied equally. The latter is especially relevant in terms of carbon accounting. The practice of carbon accounting involves translating GHG emissions into an internationally recognized measurement of CO_2 equivalents expressed as metric ton (Mt) CO_{2e}. GHG accounting quantifies and organizes information about GHG emissions based on common standards and protocols and attributes emissions correctly to a facility, company, nation, or other entity.

Accurately measuring carbon emissions is the essential prelude to developing viable decarbonization strategies that truly work.

The European Union has its own laws and agencies that set climate crisis goals. The *Regulation on the Governance of the Energy Union* sets rules for planning, reporting, and monitoring. In the UK, standards from the Task Force on Climate-Related Financial Disclosures helped form the basis of International Sustainability Standards Board (ISSB) norms that the UK says it plans to follow.[5] The UK also has its SECR, Streamlined Energy and Carbon Reporting.

EU climate law requires member countries to cut GHG emissions by 55% (compared with 1990 levels) by 2030, and achieve net zero by 2050. To fund those ambitious goals, the EU committed to spending 30% of its long-term budget for 2021–2027 and Next Generation EU for climate-related projects.[6]

ISSB Debuts Its Baseline

In June 2023, the ISSB issued its first IFRS® Sustainability Disclosure Standards—IFRS S1 General Requirements for Disclosure of Sustainability-Related Financial Information and IFRS S2 Climate-Related Disclosures. The goal of these standards is to develop a global baseline for sustainability reporting.

In today's global marketplace, where cross-border transactions are the norm, these standards mean consistent, comparable, and verifiable information about a company's exposure to and management of sustainability-related risks and opportunities.[7]

However, these standards aren't enforceable unless a particular jurisdiction, as in a country or region, endorses them, which is currently picking up momentum. The ISSB standards build on the framework from other organizations, including the UK's Taskforce on Climate-Related Financial Disclosures, the Sustainability Accounting Standards Board, and the GHG Protocol. The emergence of ISSB should not be a major concern to various reporting standards. For example, the EU's Corporate Sustainability Reporting Directive (CSRD) goes beyond the ISSB requirements.

SEC Climate Rule

The US Securities and Exchange Commission (SEC), a US government agency that is responsible for regulating the securities markets and protecting investors, is also heeding consumers' concerns for better sustainability data. Investors want transparency about climate-related risks so they can make informed investment decisions.

In March 2022, the SEC announced its Climate Disclosure Proposal, a set of regulations that require publicly traded US companies to disclose climate-related information in their financial filings. That information includes GHG emissions, climate-related financial risks, and governance structures.[8]

After nearly two years, the long-awaited proposal passed in March 2024 and became a final rule. The Enhancement and Standardization of Climate Related Disclosures for Investors mandates climate-related information in its registration statement and periodic financial statements including the following items:

- Climate-related risk and material impact on the business strategy
- Governance of climate-related risk and relevant risk management processes
- Material GHG emission of Scope 1 and 2, which for accelerated and large accelerated filers, would be subject to assurance
- Certain climate-related financial statement metrics and related disclosures in financial statements
- Information about climate-related targets and goals and transition plans, if any

These disclosures are crucial to understand a business's exposure to climate-related financial risks and to measure, identify, assess, and manage these risks.[9]

Even though Scope 3 was not mandated by the SEC, other jurisdictions will require all three scopes to be disclosed including the California Climate Policies or the EU CSRD.

To explain, Scope 1, 2, and 3 emissions are different classifications for various types of emissions from direct and indirect sources within an organization:

- **Scope 1.** Direct emissions from an organization's owned operations, including company-owned vehicles and buildings
- **Scope 2.** Indirect emissions from purchased electricity, steam, heating, and cooling
- **Scope 3.** All other indirect emissions generated throughout an organization's value chain

The SEC climate ruling is a step in the right direction as the US adopts its own standard into law, which drives global harmonization. Companies must quickly turn their attention to compliance and data integrity adherence, which often takes time and resources. At the heart of the matter; this is just the start of the decarbonization journey.

The Missing Piece

With all the organizations, statements, treaties, concerns, and catastrophes related to climate, and the facade or appearance that everyone wants to see change happen, why is our climate still in crisis?

The answer goes back to where this book began—the capitalist consumerism that drives the shift in our planet's climate in the first place. Mix that with politics, confusions, and controversies on everything from emissions activity measurements to compliance, control, and so much more.

The bottom line is that the world *is* paying attention and doing something about it. As you've read, many individual, government, and corporate sentiments have shifted from unbridled consumption in pursuit of profits to acute concern. That has forced governments of those stakeholders to pay attention to their constituents and take action—just not enough, fast enough.

US GHG emissions dropped almost 2% in 2023. That's still far short of what's needed to meet the Paris Agreement–stipulated 2030 goal of cutting GHGs globally by 55%.[10]

Public and Private Partnerships

The synergy of public and private interests converging in a capitalistic economy will lead to the development of innovative and dramatic solutions. Corporate governance as well as governments play a pivotal role often in spearheading these partnerships with the goal of bolstering progress toward climate solutions.

The World Bank, for example, works with public and private partnerships to help countries assess their carbon footprints and plans for the climate crisis. In Vietnam, they're implementing a digital platform related to public investment management across the Mekong region.

This tool enables the adoption of digital climate change screening through a reformed Public Investment Law and Construction Law, the implementation of climate vulnerability and risk assessments to inform investment decisions, and includes capacity building to institutionalize geospatial screening for climate risk.[11]

In the Middle East, the World Bank supports Jordan's establishment of a climate change unit within the Ministry of Finance to strengthen the government's response domestically and internationally.[12]

Private sector partnerships also make a positive difference. In 2020, global technology leader Google set a goal of operating its data centers and office campuses with 24/7 carbon-free energy by 2030. As part of that pledge, a year later the company partnered with clean-energy startup Fervo to develop an enhanced geothermal power project in the Nevada desert. Using new techniques, including one first developed by the oil and gas industry, the project called for tapping into Earth's consistent subsurface heat to generate electricity without burning fossil fuels or releasing carbon into the atmosphere. In November 2023, the geothermal power production facility came online.[13]

Google, continuing its efforts to expand the use of geothermal power as a viable clean-energy alternative, more recently partnered with Project InnerSpace, a nonprofit organization focused on the global development of geothermal energy. "We see significant potential for geothermal technology to provide 24/7 carbon-free energy at scale," Maud Texier, Google director for clean energy and decarbonization, said in making the partnership announcement in September 2023.[14]

Earlier in 2023, geothermal gained more support as an alternate source of renewable energy with a US Department of Energy $165 million Geothermal Energy from Oil and Gas Demonstrated Engineering grant (GEODE) awarded to a consortium that includes Project InnerSpace, the Society of Petroleum Engineering International, and Geothermal Rising. Money from the grant will be used to accelerate the growth and development of geothermal, leveraging expertise, technologies, and methods from the oil and gas industry.[15]

Another partnership that's already well on the way to delivering on a sustainable energy future is the recently completed first phase of the Dogger Bank Wind Farm, off the northeast coast of England in the North Sea. The four-phase project is a collaboration with among three companies: Equinor, SSE Renewables, and Vårgrønn.

When all phases are fully operational, the wind farm is expected to generate enough electricity to power 6 million homes a year. "This is exactly how we should respond to the energy crisis," said SSE Chief Executive Alistair Phillips-Davies, after Dogger Bank phase one went into operation. SSE is a UK-based electricity network company engaged in renewables.[16]

Vårgrønn is a Norwegian wind energy company. Further reflective of changes for the future, Norway-based Equinor is better known for its oil and gas. The company is responsible for 70% of Norway's oil and gas production.[17] But the company also has pledged that 50% of its investments by 2030 will go to renewables and low-carbon markets, and that it will cut emissions in its operated fields by 50%.[18]

Subsidies and Penalties

Governments also provide subsidies to companies and individuals with the goal of encouraging environmentally sound practices including the reduction of carbon emissions. At the other end of the spectrum, governments levy fines or penalties, as a form of oversight and reinforcement in the sustainability space.

Whatever the tool governments use, the goal should be to promote a more sustainable practice for each business as yet one more part of the multifaceted climate solution.

Cap-and-Trade Systems

A number of countries and other government entities look to carbon emissions trading as a common way to curtail emissions. Also known as cap-and-trade or allowance trading, the system has two main elements, a limit (or cap) on pollution, and tradable allowances equal to the limit that authorize allowance holders to emit a specific quantity (one ton, for example) of the pollutant. This limit helps an entity meet its environmental goal and the tradability of allowances offer flexibility on the path to compliance. Allowances are bought and sold in a marketplace.[19]

Carbon trading programs lay out the environmental goals, complying with the 1.5°C temperature increase as set by the Paris Agreement, for example, then set maximum limits on the amount of pollution a source can emit into the environment. Those limits can be reduced over time. If the source exceeds the limit, they can face stiff fines.

China and South Korea set a price on carbon and cap the total GHGs that can be emitted by certain sources. If a company doesn't pay the cost or fee for its excess emissions, or has exceeded its emissions allowance, the company faces significant fines.[20]

The Acid Rain Program of the US Environmental Protection Agency (EPA), for example, is a cap-and-trade program that's been in place for decades. Each allowance—awarded for free and at auction—authorizes a source to emit one ton of sulfur dioxide (SO_2). The affected source, like a power plant, determines how to use the allowance, whether for compliance, trade it at auction, or save it for future compliance needs.[21]

An advantage of these types of programs is their flexibility. Organizations have options for how to achieve specific environmental goals. Sometimes that can lead to achievement of a goal ahead of schedule because an organization will overcompensate upfront.

The Electric Vehicle Subsidy Lesson

Subsidies and incentives can be powerful tools. Government intervention, though, isn't always for the best as indicated by the trillions of dollars in incentives funneled to the fossil fuel industry every year. Clean energy incentives also can backfire. Plenty of government entities offer incentives for purchase, trade-in, and use of electric vehicles (EVs) with the goal of cutting down fossil fuel-related emissions.

As I mentioned previously, Norway is an excellent example of that. With the help of subsidies that have included sales tax exemptions and other freebies, almost 21% of all passenger cars in Norway are battery electric vehicles (BEVs or EVs). For the first time, though, in 2023 Norway plans to implement a VAT (value-added tax) on some BEVs and a new weight tax on all EVs.[22]

EVs tend to outweigh the more traditional internal combustion vehicles due to their battery weight, though EVs use lighter materials. An interesting fact that perhaps helps us better understand the continued prevalence of fossil fuels: gasoline or diesel fuel produces 40 times as much energy pound for pound as a state-of-the art electric battery.[23]

That's one more challenge capitalism-fueled innovation will have to solve in the coming years as batteries become more efficient.

Right now, though, Norway's government struggles to deal with the unfettered push to EVs with subsidies and few limitations. That's because there are negative consequences with EVs. Public transit has suffered; Norway has one of Europe's lowest public transport use rates. That's a negative because another important tool to reduce emissions and enhance urban lifestyles is the use of public transportation. All those EV subsidies and tax breaks also have widened the country's wealth gap, with most subsidies going to the affluent. The subsidies also didn't extend to e-bikes or golf carts, both of which have the potential to further reduce the number of vehicles on roads.[24]

When it comes to EV incentives in the United States, buyers of eligible EVs can get up to $7,500 in federal tax credits thanks to the Inflation Reduction Act of 2022. However, the number of EV models that actually qualify for the subsidies dropped dramatically on January 1, 2024—from 43 if delivered between April 18 and December 31, 2023, to just 19 models. Not all vehicles in a particular model are eligible for the rebate either. EV makers like Audi, BMW, Cadillac, Mercedes, Nissan, VW, and Volvo dropped off the list, and others like Chevrolet and Ford saw three of their EV models lose eligibility. Even Tesla lost one model. But Rivian saw three models added to the list.[25]

The reason behind the switch relates to the origin of various components and location of assembly. Says the IRS, "any vehicle with certain components assembled by a foreign entity of concern is not eligible."[26] Once again politics affects environmental decisions.

Worth noting, though, as mentioned previously in the chapter, removing all fossil fuel-powered vehicles from the roads alone isn't enough to solve our planet's CO_2 problems. The answer is always multipronged and dependent on each use case.

Sorting Through the Incentives

These are just a few of the many types of incentives (and penalties) public and private entities globally hope will accelerate the quest to overcome the climate crisis. The scope and implementation of incentives and penalties change regularly, too.

With all these opportunities for entities to address sustainability and climate crisis, analysis of the pros and cons of incentives and potential fines is essential before making decisions that affect business operations. The goal, after all, is to develop winning strategies, minimize risk, and maximize benefit.

Capitalist Economics

All of this reminds me of economists Friedman's and Smith's teachings on capitalism discussed in Part I. Both men believed that government intervention should be limited and that capitalist markets should be allowed to operate freely with the power to correct themselves.

What either person might think of our climate crisis and governance attempts to overcome its challenges, we can't know for sure. Governments, with the help of stakeholders, can, however, learn from past shortcomings when it comes to attempts to reach net zero and evolve their own policies, rules, regulations to achieve a more supportive and effective solution.

Case in point: Although the US federal government hasn't yet provided e-bike incentives, some local and more than 20 state governments recognize the value of those types of incentives in part to reduce urban traffic congestion and are considering or already offer incentives and cash-back programs for electric bicycle users.[27]

That's a lesson from others that's well learned.

Governments and Militaries

Not to be overlooked in any discussion on GHG emissions and the climate crisis are governmental organizations and their global activities, simply because of their sheer size. The US government is our country's biggest employer.

To be fair, many countries around the globe also control or quasi-control the power generation or public utilities sector. Heat and electricity generation account for 31.8% of total GHG emissions.[28]

Relationships between energy-generation plants and countries must be multifaceted, including financial and technical incentives, to create positive outcomes.

Militaries also are huge contributors to global emissions, according to a new report by Scientists for Global Responsibility and the Conflict and Environment Observatory, both UK-based nonprofits. The report estimates that the world's militaries account for 5.5% of global emissions. That includes emissions from military bases, training exercises, industrial supply chains, and the transportation of personnel and equipment. Combined, this means that global military activities are equivalent to the fourth-largest national carbon footprint in the world. And that's based on estimates of the limited, publicly available emissions data from military activities.[29]

In addition to GHG emissions, military activities can also contribute to air and water pollution. Military operations can, of course, also have negative impacts on local ecosystems and wildlife, particularly if they involve the use of hazardous chemicals or other pollutants.

The US military alone emits more GHG than entire countries like Portugal and Denmark, according to a 2018 analysis by Neta C. Crawford, a US political scientist, cofounder and codirector of the Cost of War Project, and Montague Burton Chair in International Relations at the University of Oxford. In fact, the Department of Defense accounts for nearly 80% of the federal government's fuel consumption, says Crawford.[30]

The US federal government, though, is trying to move toward sustainability one step at a time. At the end of December 2021, President Joe Biden established the Federal Sustainability Plan that lays out an approach to 100% zero emission vehicle acquisitions by 2035, including 100% light-duty acquisitions by 2027.[31]

The move by the government to lead by example with the power of procurement extends to developing a net-zero supply chain. Other elements of the plan include net-zero emissions buildings by 2045, as well as buildings powered by carbon pollution-free electricity and preparing federal agency policies, programs, operations, and infrastructure to adopt adaptive and resilient strategies for future climate impacts.[32]

Once again, the path forward to more sustainable energy is there with the help of technologies. It's simply up to all of us—public or private entities—to bring the discussions to light and take action and solve the climate challenges.

The Big Picture: A Chapter Roundup

- Typically, governments by their nature and size move more slowly to develop policies, rules, regulations, tariffs, and incentives or to foster public and private partnerships, especially when they relate to the climate crisis.
- Some countries and governments use carbon emissions trading as a method to curtail GHG emissions. Also known as cap-and-trade or allowance trading, the system has two main elements—a limit (or cap) on pollution and tradable allowances equal to the limit—that authorize allowance holders to emit a specific quantity of the pollutant.
- Another way governments encourage responsible GHG-related actions is through incentives. Not all incentives, though, end up with all positive impacts.
- Governmental organizations, including the US government, have a big effect on GHG emissions and our climate because of their sheer size. This includes not only people and organizations that directly govern but also militaries and, in some instances, power-generation systems that are fully or partially state-owned.

9

How Climate Tech Will Transform the Economy

"We are about to witness a great period of climate and energy-related innovation."

As HAS BEEN the story since the Industrial Revolution, technology will play the leading role in this next transformation of the global economy. The goal of this climate technology is to address the climate crisis by reducing greenhouse gas (GHG) emissions and helping society adapt to changing climate.

Renewable forms of energy and carbon capture/storage technologies, for example, reduce CO_2 in our atmosphere. At the same time, technologies such as sea wall defenses and improved weather warning systems help make living with the effects of climate change more manageable in the short term.

Mix of New and Old Technologies

Climate technologies, like wind power or building stilted structures in flood zones, have been around for decades. Others, like burning fossil fuels to create electricity, aren't technically climate tech;

117

nonetheless, they can contribute strategically to the overall reduction of GHG emissions.

Other technologies, like artificial intelligence (AI), satellite imagery, or data science, are more modern advancements. Satellite imagery, for example, enables agencies to monitor methane leaks or identify polluters and leaks at refineries, enhancing the monitoring and enforcement of climate laws. Also, AI enables us to work faster with consumable data at our fingertips, saving time and helping us to focus more on the core issue of decarbonization.

Fortunately, innovations in how we use new technologies like AI, machine learning, and blockchain also turn the climate crisis into a data problem. And data problems we can solve with the help of software tools that help companies and agencies accurately measure their carbon footprints and advance existing technologies in the renewable energy and weather forecasting space. Additionally, we will see AI applied to common uses like knowledge sharing of large climate datasets and energy forecasts. Ultimately, AI technology can speed up the progression of data analysis and process automation to help us reach net-zero targets faster.

New climate technologies, coupled with more traditional ones like wind and solar power, can provide solutions to stave off the worst effects of climate change on the way to net zero. For example, according to EU industry analysts, the power sector of the economy would be first to decarbonize because wind and solar power generation technologies already are in operation or available at scale.

The path to decarbonization varies across sectors. Transportation, buildings, and industry sectors are anticipated to achieve this goal sooner, while the agriculture sector faces distinctive hurdles stemming from animal production.

The Technology Disruptor

Energy will be a critical part of the decarbonization equation, whether it's about efficiencies, renewables, or something else. There also will be new services and opportunities to help with the transition from old to new and fossil fuels to alternate forms of energy.

The electrification of nearly everything imaginable will enable us to consume cleaner power at scale relatively quickly in the coming decades. The automotive industry is a perfect example of not just expanding on electrification but also on the broader concept of clean-tech innovations transforming entire parts of the economy.

Innovations from Elon Musk

Elon Musk, a market force himself, and his company Tesla provide a case study of this transformation, combining capitalism and climate to become a technology disruptor. A technology disruptor is a company, product, or service that uses new technology to fundamentally change an industry or create a new one.

Disruptors are often more efficient, convenient, and affordable than other established methods, and they can quickly capture a large market by challenging the status quo. Though not in the climate space, two other technology disruptors include Uber, which disrupted the taxi industry by using a smartphone app to connect riders with drivers, and Netflix, which disrupted the entertainment industry by streaming movies and television shows on the internet.

To better understand the role of a disruptor requires understanding the innovator's dilemma, a business conundrum that occurs when a company's success in the present becomes a barrier to its ability to adapt to new technologies or business models in the future. The term was coined by Clayton M. Christensen in his book *The Innovator's Dilemma* (2016).

The innovator's dilemma arises when a company has a strong financial incentive to continue investing in its existing products and technologies, even if those products are eventually made obsolete by newer and more innovative technologies. That can lead to the company falling behind its competitors and being unable to adapt to changing market conditions.

In 2008, several years after Musk took over the reins at Tesla, the first Tesla Roadster rolled off the assembly line. Though not the first electric car—the concept had been around for hundreds of years—the Roadster was the first premium all-electric sedan.[1]

In early 2010 Tesla debuted its first drivable model S alpha proto-type, a more affordable sedan that prepared consumers for EVs at scale. By 2012 the Model S would be available for delivery.[2] The company began the most significant period of disruption to the auto industry since its early years.

Tesla was the first to successfully manufacture and sell its premium all-electric sedans at mass scale, proving that EVs could be a modern-day viable alternative to traditional gasoline-powered cars. Not only did the company bring to market vehicles with a different fuel source than internal combustion engines, but it pioneered innovations in general automotive performance and technology. Tesla also disrupted the sales model, selling its vehicles directly to consumers, bypassing the traditional dealership model.

That doesn't mean all EV entrepreneurial startups have the same level of success as Tesla. At present Rivian Automotive, for example, founded in 2009 by entrepreneur, R. J. Scaringe,[3] still struggles and its vehicles—SUVs and high-performance trucks—remain high-priced; their average cost is about $80,000. In fact, in the third quarter of 2023, reportedly Rivian lost $30,000 on every electric truck it pro-duced, according to the *Wall Street Journal*. The reasons include lower production levels than other EV producers and high material pro-vider costs.[4]

Many consumers are willing to pay additional costs for sustainable products like Rivian. However, from a capitalism profit-oriented view-point, a company can't afford to continually lose vast amounts of money on its products and maintain long-term viability.

Lessons from Tesla

Musk and Tesla offer lessons for other companies unwilling to explore new technologies. The existing global automotive industry at the time of Tesla's early rise to fame are the archetype incumbents in the innovator's dilemma. Manufacturing cars is a complex and expen-sive process; it's not easy or inexpensive to transition factories from building internal combustion engines to EVs either. For traditional automakers, switching to EV production meant potentially disrupting revenue streams.

At the same time, startups and smaller companies like Tesla with no legacy investments in internal combustion engines are able to enter the market more easily. These companies take advantage of the fewer moving parts in EVs, and therefore can be simpler and cheaper to produce than gasoline-powered vehicles.

No matter how controversial Musk is, it's impossible to deny his contributions to climate tech. Since cofounding Tesla in 2003, he has transformed it into the most successful climate-oriented enterprise in the world. From a financial perspective, Tesla has made many people beyond Musk wealthy. That's critical because prior to Tesla, no climate-related technology company had been able to create venture-scale financial returns. Tesla has done that through strategic partnerships (like with long-time lithium-ion battery producer Panasonic), unique marketing approaches, and its willingness to try new technologies and design to develop a better product.[5] Investment successes like Tesla are important to the venture capital ecosystem because they lead to further investments and propel future opportunities for countless others.

On the technology front, Tesla's most notable contributions are to the field of energy storage. One reason EVs weren't so successful prior to Tesla was their range, as in distance, related to battery packs. (Some people, especially those who live in cold climates, might argue that's still an issue to be resolved by future technological innovations.)

Tesla's battery technology not only proved it was advanced enough to improve widespread vehicle use but also it could be scaled economically. It became the harbinger of a tsunami of mass investment in the broader energy storage category. Unfortunately, that flood of money has slowed. Investment in climate tech has been down since 2021 due to broader market trends influenced by geopolitical turmoil, economic fluctuations, inflation, and rising interest rates.

Yet one more lesson from Tesla is it proved that for green products to be competitive in the marketplace, they must create equal or greater value compared with traditional products. Musk was adamant that Tesla's vehicles must be objectively great in their own right and not just a great EV. Achieving that meant that Tesla competes, not just in a niche segment but also in the primary automotive market, capturing market share away from traditional automakers.

Scale is essential for a product or service to create tangible impact in any field. Other essentials include the following:

- **Cost.** Must be cost-effective and affordable
- **Ease of use.** Provides accessibility to a wide audience
- **Reliability.** Consistent performance to lead to user trust
- **Compatibility.** Compatible with other technologies and systems to facilitate widespread adoption
- **Regulation.** Needs to meet regulatory standards to facilitate widespread adoption
- **Marketing and visibility.** Have effective marketing and visibility to achieve widespread adoption
- **Innovation.** Offers significant improvements or benefits over existing solutions that increases adoption

Decarbonizing Technologies

Before we explore the broad realm of alternate forms of energy and the potential roles they can play in decarbonizing global industries in Chapter 9, it's important to also look at how some of the latest technologies already are making a difference.

Carbon Sequestration

As mentioned previously, organizations can compensate for their GHG emissions via carbon offsets like tree planting (biologic carbon sequestration because trees absorb carbon from the atmosphere) and carbon markets where carbon credits are traded. Both, however, can be difficult to verify and aren't necessarily permanent solutions to removing CO_2 from the atmosphere.

Geological or technological carbon sequestration, however, captures and permanently stores GHG emissions. And with new and better technologies coming on line, this type of carbon capture and removal is growing in popularity as critical decarbonization solutions.

Geological Sequestration

With geological sequestration, CO_2 is pressurized until it's liquified and then injected into underground rock formations or sinks. The idea of injecting CO_2 into underground formations isn't new. Oil and gas drillers have been doing it as part of enhanced oil recovery since the 1970s.

Until relatively recently, underground carbon sequestration has been a tough sell to businesses in general because it's costly, doesn't capture 100% of the CO_2, and it's something different. (There's that innovator's dilemma again.) That's changing, though, with the increase in stakeholder concerns about the environment and the rise of corporate risk related to climate change.

One of the big challenges with carbon capture at power plants and industrial facilities is that waste carbon dioxide is emitted mixed with other gases, and the process to extract it adds cost and energy consumption. Scientists, however, have come up with one innovative solution—a carbon dioxide filter or membrane made of graphene.

"We estimate that this technology will drop the cost of carbon capture close to $30 per ton of carbon dioxide, in contrast to commercial processes where the cost is two- to four-times higher," says Kumar Varoon Agrawal, a professor at Swiss Federal Institute of Technology Lausanne's School of Basic Sciences (EPFL Valais Wallis) and lead researcher. Agrawal and his team are now working on scaling up this approach to carbon capture in a project funded by the Swiss government and industry.[6]

The US government also has increased the business case for carbon capture with modifications to its 45Q section of the IRS tax code as part of the Inflation Reduction Act of 2022. Changes include extending the deadlines to qualify, boosting the tax credit, and easing capacity requirements for eligible projects.[7]

Carbon Casting

Graphyte, Inc., with backing from Bill Gates's Breakthrough Energy Ventures, has its own innovative approach to capturing and sequestering CO_2. The company's process, called *carbon casting*, uses readily available waste biomass, including from timber and farming operations, that it dries and compresses into dense carbon blocks surrounded by impermeable, environmentally safe barriers that are then stored in monitored underground sites.

The company claims its carbon casting "preserves nearly all the carbon captured in the biomass and consumes very little energy in the process."[8] Graphyte says its form of carbon sequestration costs less than $100 a ton and can quickly scale.[9]

Direct Air Capture

Yet another innovation to remove CO_2 from our atmosphere is direct air capture. Unlike carbon capture at the source, direct air capture technologies can happen anywhere. The CO_2 is extracted, then sequestered underground.

Current drawbacks to this approach to decarbonization include the high cost. CO_2 from ordinary air is more diluted than when it's captured at its source; therefore, it's expensive to remove and takes more energy. Another challenge is the time it takes to build facilities.

Technological Sequestration

New technologies also can provide alternatives to traditional carbon sequestration. Already in operation on a limited scale are companies that capture CO_2 and use it to make graphene, the semimetal material used for the carbon filter that's stronger than steel and touted as the material of the future. (Of note: graphene hasn't yet taken off en masse because it remains expensive to produce in pure enough form and at scale.)[10]

Another process that removes CO_2 from the atmosphere and sequesters it in another state is carbon mineralization. Mineralization is a natural process that innovators have learned to accelerate. In nature, carbon dioxide reacts with certain minerals over time— hundreds or thousands of years—to create carbonates, solid minerals, thus sequestering the carbon dioxide.

New technologies now can condense that process to hours or even years depending on the mineral composition, sources of feedstocks, atmospheric conditions, and approach used. The bottom line, though, is that an estimated up to 1 gigaton of CO_2 a year could be removed from the atmosphere if sufficient funds are invested into the research and testing of this mineralization at scale.[11]

Carbon-Injected Cement

Already under way at scale is the conversion of CO_2 waste as an element in concrete. Companies in Canada doing it include CarbonCure (Halifax, Nova Scotia) and Carbon Upcycling Technologies (Calgary, Alberta).

CarbonCure says it can retrofit its technology into existing concrete plants that enables concrete producers to inject captured CO_2 into fresh concrete during mixing. Once injected, the CO_2 reacts with the concrete mix and becomes a mineral that is permanently embedded. The company says the CO_2 mineralization increases the concrete's strength, too, resulting in economic and climate benefits. Truly a win-win solution.[12]

More Concrete News

Concrete is the second most consumed material on Earth after water. Further, production of that concrete accounts for 7% of all global GHG emissions.[13]

Now, though, there's an interim solution to the challenge, or at least a partial one. A new report from the World Economic Forum in collaboration with Boston Consulting Group with industry input from the Global Cement and Concrete Association says we can cut global GHG emissions from the use of concrete by 40% in the near term. That can be accomplished through scaled deployment in low-carbon design techniques and the use of low-carbon concrete production.[14]

The report goes on to further suggest that emissions can be significantly reduced by 2030 with three strategies:

- **Greener manufacturing.** Leveraging renewable energy sources to power processes and improving production efficiencies
- **Lower-carbon cement.** Using lower-carbon cement blends
- **Material optimization.** Implementing designs that require less cement[15]

All this sounds easy enough, but as with other sectors, the concrete industry has its challenges. According to the World Economic Forum, most design and construction firms do not consistently conduct carbon assessments for projects. Customers generally don't demand low-carbon outcomes and they're more expensive, so builders don't deliver them.

Typically, a built project is a collaboration, or lack thereof in the literal sense, across multiple independent entities. All this further complicates the ability to track, plan for, and incorporate low-carbon solutions. And, low-carbon concrete is not common practice yet.

Will concrete producers, architects, designers, engineers, and stakeholders step up and demand lower carbon emissions projects? Time will tell, but if today's ESG and finance trends are an indication of the changing culture and demands, lower-carbon concrete could become the standard operating procedure of the future.

The Big Picture: A Chapter Roundup

- Tesla offers lessons in innovation and finance that have transformed the climate tech space into a mainstream-industry-changing force.
- No matter how controversial Elon Musk is, he turned Tesla into the most successful climate-oriented enterprise in the world. Until Tesla, no climate-related technology company had been able to create venture-scale financial returns.
- The solutions to our climate crisis will come from a mix of old technologies as well as new ones, and some that haven't yet been discovered.
- Carbon sequestration, a process that's been around for decades, has gained traction as environmental stakeholders, companies, and governments demand solutions to the climate crisis.
- A natural process that removes CO_2 from the atmosphere is carbon mineralization. Now, with new technologies we can speed up the process to create carbonates, solid minerals that can be sequestered.
- More new technologies turn waste CO_2 into a resource that can be used to strengthen concrete and produce materials of the future like graphene.

10

Energy Transition

The Renewable and Clean Energy Revolution

"Electrification is an enabling factor in energy transition."

ENERGY TRANSITION—THE MOVE to alternative energy—certainly isn't new. It's been happening for centuries as humans experiment with various fuels in their quest to find a more efficient, readily available, and economical source of energy.

Burning various fuels—from cow dung to wood, whale oil, coconut oil, coal, and so on—to create fire has been widespread throughout history. Geothermal energy, the heat from inside the earth, is one of the oldest forms of renewable energy; it's sustainable, economical, and efficient; it's also dependent on geolocation as in proximity to hot springs or other geothermal sources.

Iceland, for example, relies primarily on geothermal energy because it's located in a dynamic volcanic region of the world and straddles divergent tectonic plates so that Earth's inner magma and heat are closer to the surface.[1] Taiwan is another country with access to extreme volcanic activity. In fall 2023, the Sihuangziping Pilot

Geothermal Power Plant was connected to the island's electricity grid. The plant draws on the Datun volcanoes to power its 1 megawatt generator. That's small—perhaps enough to power 1,500 households, compared with the city's overall annual power generation, which totals 6.4 million kilowatts per hour. But, it's a start and a move away from fossil fuels.[2]

And then came petroleum. Some parts of the world have used oil for hundreds of years. But as a commercially viable and readily available energy source, petroleum is relatively recent. Modern oil wells began to take shape around the 1850s—in Canada, Poland, and the United States.[3] As environmental concerns with burning fossil fuels have ramped up, though, people once again look to energy transition, this time with sustainability in mind.

The question, then, to be answered is not, "How do we accomplish this necessary transition to alternate sources of energy?" Rather, the question is, "How long will it take for better alternate sources of energy to come along en masse for us to use?"

The answer is, as you've read, not as long as you might think. With growing demands by stakeholders and more stringent government and organizational regulations, entrepreneurs and innovators already are seeing opportunities to produce better sustainable options.

Electrification Phenomenon

To understand the role of clean and renewable energy sources of the future, we first must recognize the phenomenon of the electrification of nearly everything. In our climate discussions, electrification is the process of replacing fossil fuel-based energy sources with electricity as the primary means of powered end-use technologies like transportation, heating, and cooling.

Electrification also is a factor in energy transition because it enables the integration of a wider range of clean energy sources. From an economic perspective, the main factors that determine the viability of a potential energy source scaling in relation to demand include the following:

■ **Cost.** Production of a source of energy must be competitive; that includes the cost of carbon per energy source today.

- **Resource availability.** If an energy source requires a rare or hard-to-obtain resource, it can be more costly to upscale production.
- **Infrastructure.** With infrastructure already in place, it's often easier to scale up production of energy from a particular source; that infrastructure includes what's needed to produce, transmit, and distribute that energy.
- **Government policies.** Favorable policies and incentives can make production of a new energy source more attractive.
- **Public acceptance.** Public opposition to an energy source can make it more difficult to secure the necessary approvals and financing to build infrastructure for a specific power source.

Fossil Fuels

Realistically, any discussion of energy for the future still has to include the presence of fossil fuels. We will need oil and gas for generations to come. Infrastructure replacement and unit economics dictate the need for the continual use of internal combustion engines in the form of passenger vehicles, overland trucks, airplanes, ocean vessels and generators, to name a few.

Although renewable energy sources hold immense potential as replacements for fossil fuels, integrating them into the existing energy infrastructure and overcoming energy storage efficiency and cost limitations require additional advancements to reach global scale.

Energy dependability is critical in ensuring power isn't prone to blackouts and power outages. For example, on hot summer days, power outages become more common during peak hours because the energy grid is overloaded with demand and a lack of supply. Until sufficient advancements are made on renewable energy production, ensuring full-scale grid reliability (currently) necessitates the use of primarily natural gas and coal.

Natural Gas: The Transition Fuel

Natural gas holds promise with its superior emissions profile relative to other fossil fuels, its abundance, and its broad applicability as a primary energy source. In terms of the CO_2 emissions generated from burning natural gas, about 117 pounds of CO_2 are produced per million British thermal units (MMBtu) as compared to more than 200 pounds of CO_2 per MMBtu of coal.[4] Burning natural gas releases roughly 40%–50% less CO_2 per unit of energy compared to coal.

However, the production of natural gas is not without emissions issues, specifically methane, which is a very potent GHG. It turns out that the natural gas production process can lead to much higher levels of methane released than originally believed. This is primarily through venting and leakage. So, *cleaner* might not be the best word to describe natural gas, says Mark Radka, head of the United Nations Environment Programme's Energy and Climate Branch. "But provided that methane emissions are well-managed, it's not as problematic in terms of planetary warming as coal or oil."[5] Therein lies the opportunity for natural gas to address the limitations of renewable energy at scale. As an energy provider, it is crucial to match electricity supply to consumer demand, otherwise, power outages and business disruptions would lead to economic consequences. That's where natural gas-fired peaker plants can often provide supplementary electricity production when renewable energy sources face intermittency and grid stability challenges.

When properly managed, natural gas production and use offers an intermediate solution to the transition toward a clean energy future.

Radical Twists on Old Ideas

Most *new* ideas for alternative energy sources aren't really new. They're already established energy sources that have been transformed or altered in some way to improve their efficiency, unit economics, ability to scale, and environmental footprint.

Oldest Approach to Fuel

Some of those old sources with new twists include solar, wind, nuclear, hydro, hydrogen, and even some fossil fuels. Sustainable aviation fuel (SAF), for example, discussed in Part I, uses one of the oldest approaches to creating energy—burning fats, greases, and oils, along with food and yard waste as well as woody biomass. Humans have been tossing most of that on fires to create heat and power for thousands of years.

Of course, SAF requires sophisticated, innovative production techniques to achieve its end product. But the bottom line is it's an old energy source transformed through advanced scientific innovation and creativity. Currently its use isn't widespread because of economics, but in time that will happen eventually.

Twist of Irony

On the subject of economical use of a power source, in the major oil-producing countries of the Middle East, one would assume petroleum is king in terms of their primary source of energy. Wrong!

Smart economics and common sense dictate the use of abundant renewables like solar and wind as the best options to produce energy. These countries, excluding Iran (which one easily can argue is a developing country), sell their oil and gas at a high price globally, then take their profits and invest in sustainable energy locally.

Solar arrays are everywhere, as are wind towers. That helps these countries maintain a low carbon footprint, too, all the while selling their oil and gas elsewhere at a premium.

Let's examine some of the alternative sources of energy in the world that are poised for the future in terms of real-time solutions. Some might still be conceptual, others on the drawing board, in the planning stages, in testing, or already a part of the global power grid. And, some might be crucial today, but likely to some degree will phase out tomorrow.

Solar Power

As Middle Eastern oil-producing countries recognize, magnifying or heavily concentrating the sun's rays can produce vast amounts of energy. Using the power of the sun for energy is one of the oldest sources of power, but it wasn't until 1905 that noted physicist Albert Einstein won a Nobel Prize for his discovery of photons (light particles). He predicted that at some point these particles would eject electrons, a discovery that led to modern-day semiconductor technologies.[6]

Nearly 50 years later, Bell Lab scientists developed the modern solar-electric cell. Early on its use was limited due to unit economics. Using the sun's abundant power to generate electricity and store it simply was too costly for use at scale. Gradually, though, with new engineering improvements and cost drops, solar became much more widespread.

Today, as costs continue to drop, technology changes (albeit slowly), and calls for sustainable energy increase, it's one of the fastest-growing sources of electricity.[7]

Contributing to this growth is the cost of deploying solar; it's much cheaper than fossil fuel infrastructure in terms of having to build coal- or gas-fired plants. That doesn't mean solar is without its share of challenges. The photovoltaic panels (PV), those arrays that capture the sun's energy, require huge amounts of space. The lack of availability of land can create a bottleneck. The panels currently also are manufactured primarily in China, which can lead to supply chain issues. The list of challenges goes on from there.

However, there's a push to bring greater mass PV panel production to the United States, not only to address costs and supply issues but also to cut back on greenhouse gas (GHG) emissions. If solar panel manufacturing can return to the United States by 2035, GHG emissions from the manufacture of these crystalline silicon photovoltaic panels would drop by 30%. Additionally, energy consumption would fall 13% compared with 2020, according to a recent study by scientists at Cornell University.[8]

Another long-time challenge with solar is the low conversion efficiency of PVs. Though their efficiency has dramatically improved—from just 6% with early solar modules to about 20% today—they still have a long way to go. A 20% efficiency rating means the panel can convert just 20% of the sunlight that hits it into electricity.[9]

Innovators, though, already are working on the problem. In fact, the U.S. Department of Energy's National Renewable Energy Laboratory has come up with a revolutionary solar cell with 39.5% efficiency, though it's not widely available commercially yet.[10]

The pairing of better batteries for power storage and more powerful PV panels will keep solar energy in the mix for years to come. A downside, though, is solar power needs the sun, and as a result, currently can't easily adapt to cover peak electricity demand spikes.

■ ■ ■

Solar trash creates its own issues. Those are old solar panels that are rapidly being replaced by newer, more efficient, and better ones. They have to end up somewhere, and therein lies a big problem: how to handle all the waste. Current disposal efforts are woefully lacking. In other words, right now the circular economy has not reached the solar power industry.

But one person's trash can be another's treasure. That sounds a bit corny, but it's true, especially through the lens of capitalism. Today's innovators, problem-solvers, and entrepreneurs likely will eventually come up with various solutions.

And it's not just solar trash, that's a challenge. Only 5% of electric vehicle batteries are recycled.[11] Add to that the more than 720,000 tons of decommissioned giant wind turbine blades in landfills in just the United States over the next 20 years.[12]

That's a lot of trash for alternative energies to generate. Experts and capitalism already are working on the problems.

Wind Energy

Harnessing the power of the wind certainly isn't new either. References to windmills for power date back to ancient Babylon. In more modern times, windmills evolved as a source of energy to pump water, generate electricity, grind grain, cut wood, and produce food. Like solar power, wind power needs the wind to generate electricity, so until we get better batteries for power storage, there remain struggles with peak energy demands.[13]

Some massive energy-generating installations dot the land as far as the eye can see. The largest wind farm installation in the world is in China, a country that has the global lead in wind energy production. The Jiquan (also known as Gansu) Wind Power Base at full build-out will have 7,000 wind turbines with a capacity of producing 20 gigawatts of electricity.[14]

In the United States Dwarfed by Jiquan, the largest onshore wind farm in the United States is the Alta Wind Energy Centre (also known as the Mojave Wind Farm), covering more than 32,000 acres in Kern County, California. It has 600 wind turbines and produces 1,550 megawatts (1.5 gigawatts) of electricity.[15]

Wind-generated power accounted for 22% of new electricity capacity installed in the United States in 2022, second only to solar. Impetus for this push came from governments and individual companies' clean energy goals as well as incentives from the Biden administration and advanced manufacturing production tax credits to reduce the cost of wind blades.[16]

Indicative of capitalism, though, not all proposals and plans come to fruition. For example, in early November 2023, Ørsted, a Danish multinational company, canceled its Ocean Wind I and II projects off the coast of southern New Jersey, blaming high interest rates, supply chain issues, and the inability to get the tax credits it wanted.[17]

A little over a month later, the same company, Ørsted, in partnership with US-based Eversource, won approval to build Revolution Wind, a $1.5 billion wind farm off the coast of Rhode Island.[18]

Challenges and Innovation   As I mentioned previously, wind turbine disposal is one of the biggest challenges facing the industry, especially in the United States. But new technologies are being developed and solutions evolving. Bottom lines reflect the advantages of innovations and progress, too.

Texas-based Global Fiberglass Solutions, with the help of the Composite Material & Engineering Center at Washington State University, developed what it believes is an answer to recycling decommissioned turbine blades. The company recycles the old blades into what it calls EcopolyPellets, small pellets that can be used in decking and other materials. The pellets look like tiny plastic pieces of popcorn packing material.[19]

Nuclear Energy

Japan's Fukushima and the former Soviet Union's Chernobyl disasters aside, nuclear still is very much considered an alternative power source by many parts of the world. Permitting for construction is difficult, regulations extensive, and costs high. However, countries like France derive a majority of its electricity needs from nuclear generation and have a certain level of energy independence, lessening the effects of geopolitical storms on their energy grid. Globally the United States leads in nuclear power consumption, with almost twice as much nuclear energy consumption as the next country, China.[20]

Still Controversial That doesn't mean nuclear power generation is without controversies, from protests over nuclear reactors to long delays and cost overruns with plant construction. These conflicts only add to the delays in decarbonization as different parties debate their different ideas.

Even Japan, which must import the vast majority of its energy requirements, has returned to nuclear power generation following the Fukushima disaster in 2011. The Japanese government projects 20% to 22% of the nation's power will be nuclear generated by 2030.[21]

Unquestionably, though, as a form of energy production, nuclear is a non-carbon-producing alternative energy source that has been around for generations. It will continue as an alternative energy source, too, as one more tool to help the globe reach net zero by 2050.

New Nuclear There's also a new nuclear power still in the research stages that uses nuclear reactors, but instead of uranium, the fuel is thorium. It's a new twist on something countries have talked about for a long time. In 2021, China completed its first experimental thorium-based nuclear reactor in the Goi Desert.

Thorium itself isn't a nuclear fuel. Naturally occurring thorium-232 is a fissionable material, not a fissile one, according to the International Atomic Energy Agency. That means it requires high-energy neutrons to undergo fission—splitting the atomic nuclei, releasing energy used for electricity generation. When irradiated, thorium-232 eventually forms uranium-233, which is fissile and can be used as fuel in nuclear reactors.

Advantages of thorium include it's much more abundant than uranium and can generate more fissile material than it consumes to fuel water-cooled or molten-salt-cooled reactors. Thorium also is more environmentally friendly than its uranium cousin because it generates less long-lived nuclear waste.[22]

Another Solution Microsoft founder, billionaire, and philanthropist Bill Gates has another idea for nuclear that he sees as the solution to our long-term needs. The company he cofounded, TerraPower, built its Natrium nuclear plant in Kemmerer, Wyoming, which will use liquid sodium as a reactor coolant instead of water. The big problem with water, as nuclear accidents have shown, is the pressure buildups associated with overheating that can lead to a meltdown.

The boiling point of sodium is eight times higher than water, and unlike water, doesn't need to be continually pumped through the system. The latter is another reason it's safer than traditional water-cooled reactors, if, for example, there is a power failure.

Natrium was slated for a 2030 opening. That was before geopolitics entered the picture. The plant's primary fuel source currently is made in Russia, and the Russia-Ukraine war interrupted supplies.[23] However, in late November 2023, TerraPower signed a memorandum of understanding with US-based Uranium Energy Corporation "to explore the potential supply of uranium" for Natrium and similar reactors.[24]

Fusion Future?   The US Department of Energy (DOE), along with other energy organizations around the globe, in recent years has been actively researching and developing nuclear fusion as another potential source of clean, reliable energy, no emissions, no radiation. Nuclear fusion—combining the nuclei of two or more atoms to form a new, heavier atom—is the process that powers the sun and stars.

Researchers are making progress with their experiments to create a clean form of nuclear fusion. In 2020, DOE researchers achieved the first plasma in the reactor at its San Diego experimental fusion facility. Creating first plasma means the reactor was able to generate superheated, ionized gas (plasma) that's necessary for fusion reactions to occur. This milestone demonstrates the feasibility of using fusion reactions to generate electricity.

Then in December 2022 and again in August 2023, the concept became reality. Lawrence Livermore National Laboratory achieved another first, actually producing 3.15 megajoules of fusion energy as output, exceeding the 2.05 megajoules delivered by the 192 lasers that kickstarted the nuclear fusion reaction.[25]

More recently, building on the Lawrence Livermore breakthrough, in December the DOE committed $42 million for a program that will establish multi-institutional and multidisciplinary hubs to advance foundational inertial fusion energy science and technology. The hubs will be led by researchers at Colorado State University, the University of Rochester, and Lawrence Livermore.[26]

Although all these milestones are important steps forward, nuclear fusion as a practical energy source remains an idea in experimental stages. It will likely be several decades before fusion power plants are a viable option for producing electricity.

Among the challenges, scientists need to develop a way to sustain plasma at the high temperatures and pressures required for a sustained fusion reaction. That will require advanced materials and technologies that can withstand the intense conditions. Scientists also need to develop ways to generate at scale more energy from the fusion reaction than is required to initiate and sustain the reaction.

Finally, scientists and engineers need to design and build a fusion power plant that can safely and efficiently generate electricity from the fusion reaction. This will require significant advances in the design and construction of fusion reactors, as well as the development of advanced technologies for the transmission and distribution of electricity.

Overcoming those challenges will likely take several decades. However, recent advances in fusion research suggest that we might be closer to realizing the potential of nuclear fusion as an energy source than ever before.

Hydrogen

Hydrogen could be another optimal solution—actually it could be the holy grail to our energy problems. Water—H_2O, which is two atoms of hydrogen and one of oxygen—is everywhere. Whichever innovator and changemaker figures out how to turn water into hydrogen power and do so economically at scale will change the world.

Hydrogen is an energy carrier that can store, move, and deliver energy produced from other sources. For the future, the talk is green hydrogen, energy produced from solar and stored in what's called an electrolyzer, which functions as a fuel cell in reverse because it doesn't use the power from hydrogen. Instead, water is separated into hydrogen and oxygen through electrolysis in this electrolyzer.[27]

Production   The majority of hydrogen fuel is produced by a thermal process called *natural gas reforming* and *electrolysis*. In the thermal process known as *steam reforming*, steam reacts with a hydrocarbon fuel to produce what's known as *grey hydrogen*. About 95% of hydrogen comes from steam reforming of natural gas.[28]

There's a more environmentally friendly hydrogen going mainstream: green hydrogen, made from renewable energies. I mentioned in Part I Duke Energy Florida's plans for an end-to-end 100% green hydrogen system. That Florida installation involves taking an existing solar plant and adding two electrolyzer units that will separate water molecules into oxygen and hydrogen atoms.

The resulting oxygen will be released into the atmosphere, while the green hydrogen will be delivered to safe storage. At peak energy demand, the system will deliver the stored green hydrogen to a combustion turbine that will be upgraded to run on a natural gas/hydrogen blend or up to 100% hydrogen.[29]

A big challenge with producing hydrogen on a cost-effective basis is how to do so using minimum amounts of electricity. Researchers have been working on the problem with the help of Bloom Energy and the world's largest solid oxide electrolyzer installation at NASA's Ames Research Center, in Mountain View, California. This high-temperature, high-efficiency unit produces 20% to 25% more hydrogen per megawatt (MW) than commercially demonstrated lower temperature electrolyzers.[30]

Bloom also is working on a demonstration project with Southern California Gas Company. This time it's on the campus of California Institute of Technology in Pasadena, where hydrogen will power a portion of the school's grid. The project's aim is to "showcase how leveraging existing infrastructure with electrolyzers and fuel cell technology might be able to create microgrids that deliver resilient power" in the event of power disruptions.[31]

Zero-Emissions Aviation   The concept might sound like a futuristic pipedream, but it's not. Already aviation companies are working on hydrogen electric engine-powered aircraft that are zero emissions.

England-based ZeroAvia also points to lower fuel and maintenance costs with hydrogen electric planes. The company targets 2025 for certification of its ZA600 engine.[32]

France's Airbus has its own plans to market the world's first hydrogen-powered commercial aircraft by 2035. Its ZEROe project currently is looking at various configurations and technologies. They include hydrogen combustion, which is powered by gas turbines with modified fuel injectors and fuel systems powered with hydrogen similarly to how aircraft are powered today. Another propulsion approach uses hydrogen fuel cells to create electrical energy to power electric motors that turn a propeller or fan.[33]

Yet another entrant in the hydrogen-propelled aviation space is H2Fly, a Germany-based developer of hydrogen-electric powertrain systems for aircraft. Its HY4 demonstrator aircraft, which uses liquid hydrogen to power a hydrogen-electric fuel cell system, already has completed "multiple" test flights, according to the company.

One of the big advantages of using liquid hydrogen over the gaseous version is that it can double the range of the aircraft.[34]

Hydropower

Hydropower or hydroelectric power harnesses the flow of moving water to create energy, turn turbines, and generate electricity. Additional benefits of the clean, cost-effective, and renewable energy source include flood control, irrigation support, clean drinking water, and often recreational facilities created by dam reservoirs.

Consumer sentiments these days, though, do not favor damming rivers. In fact, just the opposite; dams are being removed to restore natural ecosystems in a number of places in the United States.

Hoover Dam   Hydroelectric dams come in all sizes. In the United States, when we talk about hydropower and hydroelectricity, people often conjure up images of the giant Hoover Dam, which holds back the Colorado River to create Lake Mead on the Arizona-Nevada border. When Hoover Dam was built during the Great Depression, it was considered an engineering marvel, and still is today. Its turbines can generate 2,080 megawatts of power and serve consumers in Nevada, California, and Arizona.[35]

But, it's not the biggest of its kind in the world. That honor falls to Three Gorges Dam on the Yangtze River in China. It's not only the world's largest hydroelectric plant, but it spans 7,700 feet and can generate 22,500 megawatts of electricity. Compare that to the largest hydroelectric plant in the United States, the Grand Coulee Dam on the Columbia River, Washington, with a generating capacity of about 6,800 MW.[36]

Challenges   Other than the necessary engineering involved, the biggest challenge with hydroelectric power that relies on river flows is drought. Unfortunately, the climate crisis has made that a reality for many places around the world that look to hydropower for their electricity needs. Both Three Gorges and Hoover Dams are examples of what can happen.

Three Gorges can't produce at maximum capacity year-round.[37] Hoover Dam also has its concerns. Drought in the US Southwest, especially along the Colorado River that feeds Lake Mead, has raised the specter of what would/will happen if the water in the lake falls below the level required for water intake valves to feed the power generating plant. As a result, in 2020, an additional water intake valve at the bottom of the lake was completed to deal with the inevitable shrinking of Lake Mead.[38]

New Technologies   Pumped storage hydropower (PSH) is another renewable energy that uses two bodies of water at different elevations to generate power as the water drops from one reservoir to the other and then is pumped back up to be reused. PSH acts similarly to a giant battery because it can store power and then release it when needed. It also can be a zero-emissions process when solar power is used to pump the water back for reuse.

If that sounds a bit far-fetched, it's not—nor is it new. Pumped storage hydropower has been in use in Italy and Switzerland since the 1890s. Its first use in the United States dates to the 1930s.[39] As of 2022, approximately 96% of all utility-scale energy storage capacity in the United States involved PSH.[40]

In fact, the Los Angeles Department of Water and Power (LADWP) has considered spending billions of dollars to build a pumped hydro storage project near Lake Mead. Worried about the seemingly always short on water Colorado River, LADWP has talked about using solar and wind power to pump water from downstream back to Lake Mead where it can be stored for future power generation needs.[41]

Ocean Power

Obviously, oceans are made of water. But some of the challenges and technologies involved with harnessing the oceans' power are worth discussing separately from hydropower.

Perhaps Earth's most abundant source of energy is its oceans. There's no question it's the cheapest raw material, when you figure oceans make up more than 70% of the planet. If someone could just figure out how to create a hydrogen fuel cell that works using ocean water, that makes economic sense and is scalable. Capitalist entrepreneurs and changemakers are working on it.

The power of ocean waves alone is endless; their ebb and flow never stops. Could harnessing the power of our oceans be another of Earth's great climate saviors? Perhaps. A big problem, though, when dealing with using oceans as power sources, is that, if it's not done right, the result is acid rain, destructive in its own right.

That problem also illustrates how today's energy transition differs from those of the past. This is the age of understanding what's really happening with the use of certain fuels and the unintended consequences that go with it. Whatever we do today has a real impact on the environment and people care about that. That hasn't always been the case.

Powerful Currents   In theory, oceans allow for renewable access to power on demand. The US Energy Information Administration estimates that if we used just 10% of the technically available marine energy resources in the 50 states, that could make up for 5.7% of the country's electricity generation based on 2020 numbers. That's enough electricity to power 22 million homes. Best of all, no massive fields of solar panels or towering wind turbines would be required, and there would be zero GHG emissions.[42]

Currently companies, including Swedish startup EcoWave Power and California-based CalWave Power Technologies, Inc., are involved in pilot wave-power projects off the coast of California.[43] EcoWave Power also has projects in Gibraltar, as well as the United Kingdom, Scotland, Italy, Israel, Australia, Mexico, Portugal, and Nigeria.

Capitalist Incentives   Again reflecting how the right incentives and expertise can help foster new solutions to climate challenges, the US DOE's Water Power Technologies Office invested $24.9 million in the following four different projects/trials to tap the energy power of the oceans:

- CalWave Power's xWave wave-energy converter for its PacWave South trial device can generate about 45 kilowatts of energy—enough to power about 16 homes. When storms roll in, the device autonomously drops below the surface to hide from potentially destructive waves, or operators can remotely shut it off.
- Columbia Power Technologies (C-Power) of Charlottesville, Virginia's StingRay, is designed to generate about 50 kilowatts of energy for coastal communities and isolated islands.
- DOM Inc. of Bilbao, Spain, upgraded its floating oscillating water column to harness wave energy. As waves flow in and out of the device's open chamber, the water forces air through a turbine, generating electricity.
- The Stevens Institute of Technology in Hoboken, New Jersey, honed its dual-flap floating oscillating surge wave energy converter, which can be deployed at any water depth. The converter could generate about 100 kilowatts of energy—enough to power about 35 homes.

"Wave energy could be an incredibly valuable resource for marine researchers, coastal communities, or even disaster-relief scenarios, providing backup power and clean drinking water," said Mike Lawson, who leads the NREL marine energy team.[44]

That's true, but one of the challenges with all these approaches is that whatever the product or the process, they must be able to function in the harsh and often inhospitable ocean environment, be economically feasible, and be able to scale. Again, it will happen, and sooner than one might think.

The Big Picture: A Chapter Roundup

- To understand the role of clean and renewable energy sources of the future, we first must recognize the phenomenon of the electrification of nearly everything. That's the process of replacing fossil fuel–based energy sources with electricity as the primary means of powered end-use technologies like transportation, heating, and cooling.
- Fueled by technology improvements and decreasing costs, solar is one of the fastest-growing forms of renewable energy globally.
- Most *new* ideas for alternative energy aren't really new; they're already established energy sources that have been transformed or altered to improve efficiency, unit economics, ability to scale, and environmental footprint.
- SAF uses one of the oldest approaches to creating energy— burning fats, greases, and oils, along with food and yard waste as well as woody biomass.
- Nuclear energy produced using water-cooled reactors remains a viable alternative to burning fossil fuels to produce energy globally. But there are new types of nuclear on the drawing boards, too, including nuclear fusion and liquid sodium–cooled nuclear reactors.
- Green hydrogen could hold a key to zero-emissions aviation in the form of hydrogen electric engine–powered aircraft.
- The world's oceans could be the savior when it comes to renewable energy. The US Energy Information Administration estimates that using just 10% of the technically available marine energy resources in the 50 states would be enough to power 22 million homes.[45]

11

A New Hope

Our Changing Culture

"Sunlight is the best disinfectant. The more truth that is applied to climate issues the better chance we have to positively affect it through capitalism."

FINDING SOLUTIONS TO reversing climate change can't happen overnight. It won't be easy either; transforming a culture never is. But with capitalism and its power of innovation and transformation at the forefront and backed by strong governance, change for the better will happen and we will all come out victors.

Unbridled consumerism eventually will give way to thoughtful sustainability. Our culture of take-make-dispose will be replaced with circularity or options that better support a more sustainable environment.

All this *is* certain because the climate technology renaissance has already begun. You've read in these pages how stakeholder capitalism has fueled this awakening, how innovators and changemakers have stepped up with their ideas to address environmental problems, how venture capitalists have provided the financing, and how new twists on old ideas *are* making a difference.

Companies, organizations, and even government entities increasingly have established decarbonization targets and made climate-positive pledges. Though many of those pledges remain fluid in terms of achievement, the commitments have been made. Standardized guidelines for greenhouse gas (GHG) emissions are in place or awaiting implementation. And, most important, the financial support is there, growing every year to meet the demands of nascent climate technologies that can help solve the challenges.

Fixing our climate's problems is like starting a weight-loss plan. Once you're committed, there will be ups and downs on the journey, some good days and some not so good, and missed goals. But there are unexpected achievements, along with new challenges that will arise. Yet if you actively work on your goal and stay the course, there will be progress in the right direction.

Reporting Standardization

Using the weight-loss analogy, one of the first steps to measuring and achieving success is to create a baseline starting point and an end target. In the business context, that means a logical starting point is adopting a baseline and then developing a methodology to understand and compare results.

A good parallel from the past is the Sarbanes-Oxley Act of 2002 (SOX). That US law, which came about following high-profile cases of questionable and fraudulent accounting practices, set stringent guidelines for financial auditing and accounting at public companies.[1]

A provision of SOX was the creation of the Public Company Accounting Oversight Board, responsible for overseeing the auditing of publicly traded companies. SOX also introduced stricter rules for the certification of financial statements by corporate executives and established harsher penalties for financial fraud and misrepresentations.

It wasn't until after SOX's implementation that the principles of capitalism really took over. Entrepreneurs and changemakers created new tools to support organizations becoming more transparent with their financial data to boost investor confidence and build better internal governance through services and software to streamline and simplify compliance with the law. More than two decades later SOX is the standard operating procedure.

Sound like a familiar pattern? The same will happen with climate disclosures and carbon accounting practices that set the measurements and baseline for entities to follow.

One Step at a Time

The idea might sound a bit overwhelming, but it's not really, especially if you break down what has to be accomplished into simple steps, and take them one at a time in the right order. Keep in mind, too, there are plenty of climate technologies and partners that are available to help with every step of the process.

For example, here's carbon accounting in five easy steps:

1. Establish initial parameters like organizational boundaries and a governance strategy.
2. Identify emissions sources and collect data.
3. Align with the relevant reporting standards.
4. Create a climate strategy.
5. Report your carbon footprint.

Food Choices in a Changing Climate

Beyond the business-related side of climate change, our personal choices absolutely make a difference for our climate. Often overlooked or only an afterthought in discussions about GHGs and climate change are the foods we eat.

In fact, the foods we choose to consume can contribute substantially to GHG emissions and climate change—or not. After the production of energy, agriculture is the second largest global producer of GHG emissions.[2]

Here are a few of the ways agriculture contributes to climate change:

- The digestive process of cattle adds to methane emissions.
- Fertilizers like nitrous oxide used for crop production give off GHGs in the atmosphere and increase global warming.
- Forests, which provide natural carbon sequestration, are cut down to expand farmland.
- Other agricultural emissions come from manure management, rice cultivation, burning of crop residues, and fuel use on farms.[3]

According to the World Resources Institute, beef production accounts for the most emissions.[4] Some large hotels have giant, meat-based buffets, which could result in a large carbon footprint. The same can be said about major hospitals and their massive cafeterias that feed patients and staff members daily.

No Easy Answers

However, once again before passing judgment against cows, there's more to the numbers. Though there's no question cattle are big producers of methane, it's important to note that the gas cows produce is biogenic methane, which differs in its global warming characteristics from fossil-fuel produced methane, according to researchers at the University of California–Davis. Biogenic methane comes from cows eating grass or feed containing CO_2 absorbed from the atmosphere. Burning fossil fuels creates new gas emitted into the atmosphere. The biogenic methane eventually returns to the atmosphere as recycled carbon.[5]

More UC Davis researchers point to the fact that cows and other ruminants account for only 4% of US GHG emissions, with beef cattle only 2%. Those same researchers are looking at innovative ways to reduce methane emissions in livestock through improved breeding, genetics, and especially nutrition.[6]

That's only in the United States. Globally, livestock emissions are a much bigger issue. Livestock account for 14.5% of GHG emissions. Keep in mind, though, India has the largest cattle population but the lowest beef consumption.[7]

Just as with climate change itself, there are no easy answers, and no one single silver bullet to solve all the challenges.

Plant-Based Options

So many industries contribute to our planet's GHGs; agriculture is no different. But also as with other industries, new technologies and efficiencies in production can and do make a difference not only in the final products but widespread acceptance and use.

With the foods we eat, innovation and alternative foods offer yet another hope. Tofu as a meat alternative has been around literally for thousands of years. Reportedly the Chinese originated it, though the dates are vague.[8] Various other meat substitutes have been around for centuries, including tempeh (made with fermented soybeans), which originated in Indonesia, and seitan (wheat gluten), also with origins in China.

Since early in the 20th century, other vegetarian protein alternatives have been manufactured by various organizations, including Loma Linda Foods in Loma Linda, California. But it's only been more recently that plant-based meat alternatives have gone mainstream. Brands like Tofurky, Boca Burgers, Gardenburgers, Impossible Burgers, and more account for veggie burgers, quinoa burgers, and various other meat alternatives.[9] The size of the plant-based meat market topped $13.6 billion in 2023 with estimates it will reach $87.9 billion by 2032.[10]

Laboratory or cultivated meat debuted in 2013 when a team led by Dutch pharmacologist Mark Post at Maastricht University introduced the first cultivated burger. Post also is cofounder of Mosa Meat, a cultivated-meat company.[11] The cultivated-meat market remains in its nascent stages, and is expected to be a $25 billion global industry by 2030. Reaching just 1% of the global protein market would require significant financial investments in the tens of millions. Stay tuned for further developments in this emerging industry as it has the potential to revolutionize the meat landscape.

The bottom line is that as consumers, we now have alternative choices that can foster a more sustainable future for our food system.

Power in Paradise

The state of Hawaii offers a prime example of how a climate-positive frame of mind, breakthrough technologies, and the power of stakeholder capitalism can join forces for change—this time in the energy sector.

Despite the abundance of wind and sun in the Hawaiian Islands, for generations burning fossil fuels like coal and oil have been the state's primary source of energy. Because coal and oil must be shipped to the islands, that adds to the environmental impact. Hawaii also has the highest electricity retail prices in the United States, nearly triple the US average, according to numbers from the US Energy Information Agency.

But things have begun to change for the better. The state plans that 100% of its electricity will be from renewable sources by 2045. As of 2022, 29% came from renewables.[12]

One of the challenges with an all renewable-energy grid is electricity storage capacity. After all, the sun doesn't always shine even in Hawaii. But thanks to Tesla's megapacks, a commercial grade lithium-ion battery that can store 3.9 MWh of energy—enough to power 3,600 homes for an hour[13]—the challenge has been addressed.

As of January 11, 2024, Kapolei Energy Storage on Oahu was up and running, and connected to the island's power grid. According to Plus Power, which owns and operates the battery system, it's "the most advanced grid-scale battery energy storage system in the world" and will help transition the state's electric power from coal and oil to solar and wind.[14]

The Importance of Leadership and Action

Hawaii's energy paradigm reflects that the increased transparency and awareness growing among consumers inevitably encourages responsible consumption and demands more investments in cleaner energy. Capitalism provides the framework to conquer the challenges of the climate crisis. Also crucial is corporate and governmental leadership that can often help set the tone and take the lead in highlighting our environmental challenges.

There's a fine line between profits and sustainability. Today we are at the tipping point where these two, working together, can collide and enable capitalism to prevail, driving a new era of clean energy and sustainable consumption.

Governments look to business leaders to help set the agendas, and not just in terms of talk, pledges, and verbal commitments, but in tangible actions that affect communities and global stakeholders. Walmart is an example of a company that has embraced sustainability and uses its power of procurement to influence its suppliers to follow suit.[15] Amazon does the same.

When a leader takes the initiative to understand their organization's impact on the environment, positive change can happen. Leaders strategize with their teams to determine how to cut emissions, make sustainable investments that challenge the status quo, and embrace circularity for a better future. This level of change will most likely overflow beyond their company and into their communities, geographic regions, and eventually around the globe.

The climate crisis has created countless physical and economic problems and challenges for the world, some of which exist today and many of which are yet to manifest in the future. Where problems exist in a free market opportunity, market forces will align enterprises to create solutions in the pursuit of profits. This will usher in a period of great innovation and wealth creation as entrepreneurs, investors, and governments align to deploy the capital and build the goods and services that are critical to solve climate change. Innovations across technology, economic, and political systems will drastically cut new emissions and eventually lead to declining GHG levels in our atmosphere.

Although I am optimistic that these solutions will become reality, timing is crucial to avert catastrophic impact on our planet and humanity. My hope is that this book can help guide you to be part of the solution in your personal life, business interactions, and beyond. And, with some of the ideas in these pages you now have a better understanding of the economic causes in conjunction with scientific ones, and, most important, what we can and are doing to fix our climate crisis.

Ultimately, I hope you bring the resources available to you to help us advance the critical solutions that offer the best hope to ensure our planet is not just habitable, but thriving for our lifetime and humanity's future lifetime.

Addendum I

My Climate Journey

I believe the world will rise to the challenge to solve the climate crisis. Actually, I'm a sellout to the idea, as CEO of Persefoni AI Inc., a climate-tech software company that enables companies to measure and report their climate activity. However, sustainability has long shaped the way I think and view the world.

I was born in Japan to a Japanese father and German mother. I've always been closely connected to nature in part because of my Japanese heritage. The Japanese revere nature and the sea, and it plays a role in nearly every aspect of life on the island.

My parents divorced when I was young, and my mother returned to Germany with me in tow. We remained there until my middle-school years living in a predominantly agricultural region not far south of Frankfurt. Though my family didn't farm, farming defined the community. The outdoors, animals, and nature were part of my life.

Growing up, the German cultural emphasis on valuing resources stemmed, in part, from the fear and experience of scarcity. At the time, it was forty-plus years after World War II, but the older generations, our grandparents, had grown up with little, and remembered the struggles. Sustainability and recycling were ingrained as a necessity in life and in fact struck into law throughout the country.

Then my mother married again; this time to a US serviceman, and off we went to the United States, the Deep South—rural Alabama. Compared with the Germany I knew, this was the land of plenty . . . and a massive culture shock. Sustainability and recycling weren't part of the vernacular back then in Alabama.

Another shock for me was when my stepfather, who grew up in a coal mining family in West Virginia, took us back there to visit. I remember being awestruck by the pristine beauty of some of the most incredible forests and mountain country, and then shocked by the mining and timber activities that left mountainsides cleared of forests and then the mountains literally excavated away for their minerals. My mother had always talked about the destruction of the environment and cruelty to animals; the visuals in West Virginia were a stark reminder.

We eventually moved out West to New Mexico and later to Arizona. Going from green forests to desertscapes was yet another adjustment. But today I love desert ecosystems and have come to appreciate their beauty in a way that can only be experienced first-hand. Living sustainably in deserts at scale is another story entirely.

As you can probably understand by now, an inhabitable planet with its natural beauty intact matters to my family and me.

Let me fast-forward through my career with roles of accelerating responsibility at Insight Enterprises (NSIT), Software One (SWON), Accenture (ACN), and Chesapeake Energy (CHK). At Chesapeake Energy I struggled with the thought of working for a major oil and gas company, nonetheless I approached the job in the same fundamental way I approach all challenges: one cannot begin to solve a problem until one thoroughly measures and understands it, and understanding requires data.

In 2017, Chesapeake offered me the role of chief digital officer to succeed the retiring chief information officer, who was my primary executive stakeholder at the company. The job entailed managing hundreds of employees and contractors, managing the company's entire IT estate, and leading its modernization efforts as part of a broader digital transformation strategy that I had led the development of while at Accenture.

The idea of working at a "fracking" company also bothered me. Fracking, vernacular for hydraulic fracturing, is a drilling and well completion technique that's drawn controversy in recent years. The fracking process dates back to the mid-20th century, and is the high-pressure injection of liquids and materials into the ground to force small fractures and extract more oil and gas. In the United States alone, fracking has been used in more than 1.7 million wells.[1]

Then I asked myself, why am I struggling with accepting the job at Chesapeake? As an entrepreneur I have a natural tendency to go against the grain. This dates back to my high school years, as a senior in Albuquerque, New Mexico, when I shadowed a state senator for a day as part of a political science project. I chose one of the oldest and most conservative state senators in the caucus because I wanted to better understand the *other* side so that one day I could better effect political change. Although I didn't come away from that experience with a bigger appreciation of the senator's conservative beliefs, the exercise reminded me that I can learn from those whom I don't understand.

Immediately after being faced with this decision to work at Chesapeake, I reached out to my good friend and contributor to this book, Russ Mitchell. Russ is the consummate promoter and someone I can always count on to shoot me straight. He naturally told me I'd be foolish to turn down such an opportunity, but more important, he helped me realize why I had to take the job.

It was at that moment that I connected the dots and realized three things:

- I had become part of the chorus of voices happy to complain about the "bad" and thinking that simply exercising my voice was enough.
- I was already justifying my work as a consultant helping these companies use data and systems to operate more responsibly, and thus reducing the negative impact they had on the environment and other stakeholders.
- I had faced this conundrum before.

I could argue now that potentially all I was doing was helping those companies produce more of whatever polluting product they were producing without being more environmentally responsible.

I decided to take the job as the CDO at Chesapeake. To those unfamiliar with Chesapeake, it was one of the most influential companies in the world ushering in the shale revolution.

The shale revolution, also known as the shale boom or shale gas revolution, was a period of rapid development and expansion of the shale oil and shale gas industry that began in the mid-2000s and continued into the 2010s. It was marked by the widespread adoption of new technologies, like horizontal drilling and hydraulic fracturing, which made it possible to extract oil and natural gas from shale formations that had previously been considered quite difficult or costly to access.

All this had a significant impact on global energy markets because the increased production of shale oil and gas led to a significant boost in global supply of these resources and a corresponding decline in prices. It also had economic and environmental implications, as the expansion of the shale industry created new jobs and economic opportunities in some areas, but also raised justified and very valid concerns about the environmental impact of the drilling and fracking processes. Overall, the shale revolution was a significant shift in the global energy industry and had far-reaching economic and environmental consequences.

It's also where I first saw the investor class ramp up pressure on organizations to provide transparent carbon emissions reports.

At this point, my life's puzzle fell into place—from my childhood where sustainability was omnipresent to my professional experience with software, data, and digital transformation. I was fortunate to be at the right place at the right time as by 2019, the global market for digital solutions to emissions reporting was about to explode.

It was the greenhouse gas (GHG) emissions reporting version of the technology gold rush following the Sarbanes-Oxley Act (SOX) of 2002. With the implementation of SOX, as at the time with GHG reporting, most enterprises had no technology tools to manage the need.

Virtually no enterprise had off-the-shelf carbon accounting software designed for investor-grade reporting with internal controls for data, function, and processes. Software to treat your climate data/ transactions with the same rigor and confidence as your financial transactions.

In 2019, I gave up my career with Chesapeake to create a climate technology company and build a category to support this demand. Partnering with my friends and cofounders Jason Offerman and Kim Stroh, we created Persefoni, a climate software-as-a-service business that develops tools to enable companies and financial services around the world to more clearly understand and manage the impact they have on our planet. By January 2020, Persefoni was fully operational and incorporated, and it has rapidly evolved into what we refer to as the ERP of Climate™ (ERP is an acronym for enterprise resource planning).

Since then, we've achieved an amazing level of market leadership. Many around the world consider Persefoni one of the top companies in this space, and depending on whom you ask, they may even tell you that we're the best at what we do.

Along the way we've been very fortunate to have our team and work featured in countless press articles and recognized by globally renowned business and entrepreneurial programs including Fast Company's Most Innovative Companies for 2023, SXSW, EY Entrepreneur of the Year Finalist in 2022, and Forbes 30 Under 30.

I share all of this not as a point of hubris but to highlight the fact that climate tech has reached mainstream in the business world. Even more significant to the context of this book, we have accomplished our successes serving investors and capital providers, both the lifeblood of the capitalist system.

It's been a whirlwind five years since I embarked on this climate tech path. What I've learned and been able to accomplish in the realms of capitalism, energy, and climate since then would have been impossible to replicate without having been on the inside of the machine.

It's with this experience that I share with you my thoughts on the importance of us embracing the right parts of an evolved capitalism to drive systemic change at a global scale.

Addendum II

For More Information

Climate leadership: https://www.epa.gov/climateleadership

Corporate climate action: Science-Based Targets Initiative. https://sciencebasedtargets.org

Company disclosure: The Carbon Disclosure Project (CDP). https://www.cdp.net/en/companies-discloser

Greenhouse gas emissions and sinks: https://www.epa.gov/ghgemissions/inventory-us-greenhouse-gas-emissions-and-sinks

GHG Inventory Development Process and Guidelines: US EPA https://www.epa.gov/climateleadership/ghg-inventory-development-process-and-guidance

Greenhouse Gas Protocols: Greenhouse Gas Protocol Corporate Standard. https://ghgprotocol.org/sites/default/files/standards/ghg-protocol-revised.pdf

ISSB: International Sustainability Standards, (also IFRS/International Financial Reporting Standards). https://www.ifrs.org

SEC Climate-Related Disclosure Rule: https://www.sec.gov/rules/2022/03/enhancement-and-standardization-climate-related-disclosures-investors

Glossary

Benchmarking. The practice of measuring and comparing ESG performance with other companies in your sector or geography to understand where your company fits among your competitors.

Carbon accounting. Quantifying and tracking the greenhouse gas (GHG) emissions produced by private and public organizations. It is a systematic process that measures the carbon emissions associated with an organization's operations, helping to identify the sources and amount of emissions they generate.

Carbon credits. Also known as carbon allowances, tradable permits or certificates that represent the offset of one ton of carbon dioxide equivalent (CO_2e) emissions. They are used in carbon markets to encourage and enable organizations to offset their greenhouse gas emissions. These credits can be bought and sold, with the goal of balancing emissions by supporting projects or activities that reduce, remove, or avoid an equivalent amount of emissions elsewhere.

Carbon footprint. An estimate of how much carbon dioxide and other greenhouse gases are produced to support your lifestyle or organization; usually expressed in terms of CO_2e.

Carbon markets. Public and private marketplaces where carbon credits are bought and sold.

Carbon neutral. Focuses on balancing an entity's carbon emissions with carbon removals, typically achieved through sustainable carbon offset programs.

Carbon offsets. Used to offset the amount of carbon that an individual or institution emits into the atmosphere; work in a financial system where, instead of reducing its own carbon use, a company can comply with emissions caps by purchasing carbon credits from an independent organization.

Carbon offtake. Direct removal and sequestering of CO_2 from the air; sequestration can be permanently underground or by technological means.

CDP. A nonprofit that runs the global disclosure system for investors, companies, cities, states, and regions to manage their environmental impacts. CDP offers reports and resources on three focus areas: climate change, water, and forests.

Climate. The average weather and patterns measured over a defined period of time.

Climate change. Increasing changes in weather patterns, precipitation, temperatures, and wind patterns over a long period.

Climate risks. Encompasses both physical risks, which are tangible consequences like flooding and extreme weather events that affect an organization's infrastructure and supply chains, and transition risks, which are related to the shift from reliance on fossil fuels and toward a low-carbon economy. Transition risks can include factors like carbon taxes, mandates for carbon disclosure, and the shift to renewable energy sources.

Consolidation. The combining of GHG emissions data from separate operations that belong to one or a group of companies.

CSR (corporate social responsibility). A voluntary way for companies to commit to ethical business practices and improve their environmental, economic, and social sustainability. ESG is a way for companies to measure their CSR.

CSRD (Corporate Sustainability Reporting Directive). A directive that mandates reporting on 10 sustainability topics, including climate-related aspects like mitigation, adaptation policies, energy use, and GHG emissions (including Scope 3), with external assurance gradually phasing in. It requires adherence to European Sustainability Reporting Standards, determined by a materiality assessment, ensuring disclosure of crucial aspects while emphasizing that materiality doesn't make the reporting voluntary.

Decarbonization. The process of reducing or eliminating carbon emissions. Total decarbonization requires eliminating the production of carbon and removing carbon currently in the atmosphere.

Emission factors. How activity data is converted into GHG emissions. GHG emissions are released into the atmosphere through economic activities or processes that emit hydrocarbons. To measure these, a carbon dioxide equivalent (CO_2e) value is given relative to the activity associated with the release of the GHG; this is known as an emission factor.

EPA (Environmental Protection Agency). An independent executive agency of the US government tasked with environmental protection matters, including emission factor sets.

ESG (environmental, social, and governance). The three pillars through which an organization's effect on the environment and society can be measured.

Financed emissions. GHG emissions that are indirectly generated as a result of investments and loans. The GHG Protocol categorizes financed emissions as "investments" in Scope 3, Category 15. For example, when an investor finances an oil and gas company, they are indirectly supporting that company's operations and subsequent emissions.

Fossil fuel. A generic term for organic material (from decayed plants and animals) that has been exposed to heat and pressure from the Earth's crust for hundreds of millions of years and converted into oil, coal, or natural gas.

Fugitive emissions. Emissions that are not physically controlled but result from the intentional or unintentional releases of GHGs. They commonly arise from the production, processing, transmission, storage, and use of fuels and other chemicals, often through joints, seals, packing, gaskets, and so on.

Geothermal energy. Electricity generated by harnessing hot water or steam from within the Earth.

GHG sink. Also known as carbon sink, this is any physical unit or process that stores greenhouse gases. This usually refers to forests and underground or deep sea reservoirs of CO_2.

GHGP (Greenhouse Gas Protocol). Created in 1997, the GHGP is the original carbon accounting standard that provides guidelines for organizations to develop greenhouse gas emissions inventories.

GHGs (greenhouse gases). Often referred to in general as carbon dioxide/CO_2, though also applies to additional types of gases.

Global warming. An average increase in the temperature of the atmosphere near the Earth's surface and in the troposphere can contribute to changes in global climate patterns.

Greenwashing. The act of companies portraying a more sustainable, ethical, or "green" image of themselves for marketing purposes

Green finance. Financing environmentally sustainable projects and activities that combat climate change and reduce emissions; can include investments in initiatives like renewable energy, energy efficiency, and conservation efforts, promoting a shift to a low-carbon economy while offering financial benefits and supporting climate goals.

GRI (Global Reporting Initiative). Founded in 1997 following public outcry over the Exxon Valdez oil spill, the GRI created the first global standards for sustainability reporting (the GRI Standards) and is today one of the most commonly used reporting frameworks, helping businesses, governments, and other organizations understand and communicate the impact of companies on critical sustainability issues.

GWP (global warming potential). Each greenhouse gas has a global warming potential, a factor that refers to its heat-trapping ability relative to that of CO_2. Because GHGs vary in their ability to trap heat in the atmosphere, some are more harmful to the climate than others.

Investor-grade reporting. Similar to financial reporting, this ensures that ESG (environmental, social, and governance) data is accurate, timely, auditable, and comparable.

IPCC (Intergovernmental Panel on Climate Change). An intergovernmental body of the United Nations responsible for advancing knowledge on human-induced climate change.

ISO 14064. An international standard for measuring and reporting greenhouse gas emissions.

ISSB. The International Sustainability Standards Board is a body established by the International Financial Reporting Standards (IFRS) Foundation in November 2021 to create high-quality sustainability standards that address investors' informational needs; standards, including IFRS S1 for general sustainability disclosures and IFRS S2 for climate-related disclosures.

Kyoto Protocol. An extension of the UNFCCC, applies to seven greenhouse gases: carbon dioxide (CO_2), methane (CH_4), nitrous oxide (N_2O), hydrofluorocarbons (HFCs), perfluorocarbons (PFCs), sulfur hexafluoride (SF_6), and nitrogen trifluoride (NF_3); commits nations to take a specific action limiting and reducing GHG emissions in accordance with agreed-on individual targets.

Materiality. Material issues are those that cannot be ignored when assessing the sustainability of a company. Materiality has now evolved to be a concept of "double materiality." Double materiality speaks to the fact that ESG issues or information can be material from both financial and nonfinancial perspectives.

Net zero. A common target for organizations to commit to by 2050 as prescribed by the IPCC; refers to negating the amount of carbon a company emits by withdrawing the same amount of carbon through offsets and having it stored permanently in carbon sinks (see carbon sequestration).

Operational boundaries. In carbon accounting, defines the scope of direct and indirect emissions within organizational boundaries; categorized into Scope 1 (direct emissions), Scope 2 (indirect emissions from purchased energy), and Scope 3 (other indirect emissions in the value chain).

Organizational boundaries. Carbon accounting determining whether an organization is a part of a larger entity or subsidiary, affecting their control over company assets and the share of emissions they're responsible for; direct emissions are those from sources owned or controlled by the company, and indirect emissions result from the company's activities but occur at sources controlled by other entities.

(The) Paris Agreement. A legally binding international treaty on climate change; aims to limit global warming to well below 1.5°C, compared to preindustrial levels.

PCAF (Partnership for Carbon Accounting Financials). Published in 2020 as a response to industry demand for a global standard, a standardized approach to measure and report financed emissions; provides detailed methodological guidance to measure and disclose GHG emissions associated with six asset classes: listed equity and corporate bonds, business loans and unlisted equity, project finance, commercial real estate, mortgages, and motor vehicle loans.

Physical risk. A type of risk caused by climate change that refers to the economic costs and financial implications resulting from climate change, such as increasing extreme weather events, severe climate shifts, and other indirect effects of climate change (e.g. water shortage).

SASB (Sustainability Accounting Standards Board). A nonprofit organization formed to create industry-based standards that help companies identify and disclose financially material sustainability information. The Financial Accounting Standards Board (FASB) and International Accounting Standards Board (IASB) have long been responsible for creating financial accounting and reporting standards. SASB aims to specifically create standards to help companies manage and disclose sustainability information that affects a company's enterprise value.

SEC Climate Rule. Affects US public companies and foreign private issuers; designed to meet investor demands for more consistent, comparable, and reliable climate-related disclosures; proposal requirements include narrative disclosures, Scopes 1 and 2 GHG emissions reporting, and Scope 3 if material or included in reduction targets (except for smaller reporting companies). Larger companies would need external assurance over Scopes 1 and 2 GHG emissions, with phased implementation.

Science-based targets (SBTs). Emission reduction goals that align with the decarbonization needed to limit global temperature increases, as defined in the Paris Agreement; aim is to hold global temperature increases below 2°C above preindustrial levels, with an encouragement to limit increases to below 1.5°C; Science-Based Targets Initiative (SBTi) provides guidance and validation for companies setting SBTs, enabling them to align their emissions reduction goals with global climate objectives.

Scope 1, 2, and 3 emissions. Categories used to classify different types of emissions within an organization.

Scope 4 emissions. Not currently an officially recognized category; refers to potential emissions reductions resulting from more efficient products or services replacing less efficient alternatives.

Sustainable Development Goals (SDGs). Seventeen interconnected goals for sustainable development set by the United Nations in 2015 with the objective that these goals be met by 2030.

Sustainable finance. Financial practices and investments that prioritize ESG factors, aiming to generate both financial returns and positive, sustainable outcomes for the planet and society.

Sustainable procurement. Process of integrating environmental, social, and governance (ESG) considerations into the acquisition of services and goods.

TCFD (Task Force for Climate-Related Financial Disclosures). Now disbanded, an industry-agnostic climate-related disclosure framework that established 11 recommendations across four key areas of interest: governance, strategy, risk management, and metrics and targets; designed to help companies provide better-quality data to support informed capital allocation decisions.

Transition risk. Caused by climate change, a risk related to the process of transitioning away from reliance on fossil fuels and toward a low-carbon economy, including shifts in climate policy, regulation of certain industries, and global market sentiment.

UNFCCC (UN Framework Convention on Climate Change). Commonly referred to as *the Convention*, its ultimate goal was to stabilize greenhouse gas concentrations "at a level that would prevent dangerous anthropogenic (meaning human-induced) interference with the climate system."

Verification. An independent assessment of the reliability (considering completeness and accuracy) of a GHG inventory.

Notes

Introduction

1. United Nations. (2023). Our growing population. https://www.un.org/en/global-issues/population (accessed 20 December 2023).
2. United Nations. (n.d.). Climate action fast facts. https://www.un.org/en/climatechange/science/key-findings (accessed 12 November 2023).
3. European Commission. (2023). Renewable energy targets. https://energy.ec.europa.eu/topics/renewable-energy/renewable-energy-directive-targets-and-rules/renewable-energy-targets_en (accessed 22 November 2023).
4. European Commission. (2023). Eurostat statistics explained. https://ec.europa.eu/eurostat/statistics-explained/index.php?title=Renewable_energy_statistics (accessed 29 December 2023).
5. European Commission. (2023). European climate law. https://climate.ec.europa.eu/eu-action/european-climate-law_en (accessed 29 December 2023).
6. COP28 UAE. (2023). COP28 presidency united the world on loss and damage. COP28 UAE press release (30 November). https://www.cop28.com/en/news/2023/11/COP28-Presidency-unites-the-world-on-Loss-and-Damage (accessed 24 January 2024).

Chapter 1

1. Da Victoria Lobo, N. (2022). What will it be: ESG or SOS? Swiss Re blog (13 July). https://www.swissre.com/risk-knowledge/risk-perspectives-blog/esg-or-sos-climate-risk.html#:~:text=According%20to%20Swiss%20Re%20Institute,slow%20to%20embrace%20the%20SDGs%3F (accessed 12 November 2023).

2. United Nations. (2023). Climate action. https://www.un.org/en/climatechange/science/key-findings (accessed 12 November 2023).

3. Copernicus Climate Change Service. (2023). 2023 on track to become the warmed year after record October. European Union (10 November). https://climate.copernicus.eu/2023-track-become-warmest-year-after-record-october (accessed 12 November 2023).

4. Global Climate Change. (2023). Global temperature. NASA. https://climate.nasa.gov/vital-signs/global-temperature (accessed 10 November 2023).

5. Goddard Institute of Space Studies. (2023). NASA announces summer 2023 hottest on record. NASA (14 September). https://climate.nasa.gov/news/3282/nasa-announces-summer-2023-hottest-on-record (accessed 12 November 2023).

6. CO_2.earth. (2023). Daily CO_2 (30 December). https://www.co2.earth/daily-co2 (accessed 31 December 2023).

7. Weart, S., and American Institute of Physics. (2023). The discovery of global warming (May). https://history.aip.org/climate/timeline.htm (accessed 12 November 2023).

8. NASA. (2023). Artic sea ice minimum extent (September). https://climate.nasa.gov/vital-signs/arctic-sea-ice (accessed 14 November 2023).

9. Moatsos, M. (2021). Global extreme poverty present and past since 1820. *How was life? New perspectives on well-being and global inequality since 1820* (Volume II). (Paris: OECD Publishing). https://www.oecd-ilibrary.org/sites/e20f2f1a-en/index.html?itemId=/content/component/e20f2f1a-en (accessed 15 November 2023); Zitelmann, R. (2020). Anyone who doesn't know the following facts about capitalism should learn them. *Forbes* (27 July). https://www.forbes.com/sites/rainerzitelmann/2020/07/27/anyone-who-doesnt-know-the-following-facts-about-capitalism-should-learn-them/?sh=1d1309433dc1 (accessed 15 November 2023).

10. Saunders, J. (2023). Florida property insurance company insolvent after losses caused by Hurricane Ian. Click Orlando (12 February). https://www.clickorlando.com/news/2023/02/17/florida-property-

insurance-company-insolvent-after-losses-caused-by-hurricane-ian (accessed 12 November 2023).

11. Deventer, C. (2023) Can lawmakers save the collapsing Florida home insurance market? Bankrate (19 September). https://www.bankrate.com/insurance/homeowners-insurance/florida-homeowners-insurance-crisis/#crisis (accessed 12 November 2023); My Florida CFO. (2023). Companies in receivership, companies in liquidation. https://www.myfloridacfo.com/division/receiver/companies (accessed 12 November 2023).

12. Straughan, D. (2023). Why car insurance companies are leaving some states. Automoblog (1 November). https://www.automoblog.net/why-car-insurance-companies-leaving-some-states (accessed 12 November 2023).

13. Canadian Interagency Forest Fire Centre. (2023). Current fires summary. https://ciffc.net/summary (accessed 12 November 2023).

14. United Nations. (2023). Hottest July ever signals era of global boiling has arrived, says UN chief (12 July). https://news.un.org/en/story/2023/07/1139162 (accessed 12 November 2023).

15. Investor.gov. (2023). Environmental, social, and governance investing. US Securities and Exchange Commission. https://www.investor.gov/introduction-investing/investing-basics/glossary/environmental-social-and-governance-esg-investing (accessed 22 November 2023).

16. EPA. (2023). Causes of climate change. (25 April).https://www.epa.gov/climatechange-science/causes-climate-change (accessed 22 November 2023).

17. Thompson, C. (2019). How 19th century scientists predicted global warming. *JSTOR Daily* (17 December). https://daily.jstor.org/how-19th-century-scientists-predicted-global-warming; UK Research and Innovation. (2021). A brief history of climate change discoveries. https://www.discover.ukri.org/a-brief-history-of-climate-change-discoveries/index.html (accessed 11 December 2023).

18. Fourier, B. (1818). General remarks on the temperature of the terrestrial globe and the planetary spaces. *The American Journal of Science* 3 (1), 1–20. https://archive.org/details/mobot31753002152103/page/15/mode/2up (accessed 22 November 2023).

19. Huddleston, A. (2019). Happy 200th birthday Eunice Foote, hidden climate science pioneer. NOAA Climate.gov (17 July). https://www.climate.gov/news-features/features/happy-200th-birthday-eunice-foote-hidden-climate-science-pioneer (accessed 12 November 2023).

20. UK Research and Innovation. A brief history of climate change discoveries. https://www.discover.ukri.org/a-brief-history-of-climate-change-discoveries/index.html (accessed 12 November 2023).

21. Ritchie, H., Rodés-Guirao, L., and Mathieu, E. (2023). Population growth. https://ourworldindata.org/world-population-growth (accessed 12 November 2023).

22. The White House (2021). New tools needed to assess climate-related financial risk (03 Nov). https://www.whitehouse.gov/cea/written-materials/2021/11/03/new-tools-needed-to-assess-climate-related-financial-risk-2/ (accessed 09 March 2024).

23. Taalbi, J. (2017). What drives innovation? Evidence from economic history. *Research Policy* 46 (8), 1437–1453. https://www.sciencedirect.com/science/article/pii/S004873331730104X (accessed 22 November 2023).

24. Tyson, A., Funk, C., and Kennedy, B. (2023). What the data says about Americans' views of climate change. Pew Research Center (9 August). https://www.pewresearch.org/short-reads/2023/08/09/what-the-data-says-about-americans-views-of-climate-change (accessed 22 November 2023).

25. IEA. (2023). World energy outlook 2023: Executive summary. https://www.iea.org/reports/world-energy-outlook-2023/executive-summary (accessed 4 November 2023).

26. European Commission. (n.d.). Renewable energy directive. https://energy.ec.europa.eu/topics/renewable-energy/renewable-energy-directive-targets-and-rules/renewable-energy-directive_en (accessed 8 November 2023)

27. Blakers, A. (2023). These four charts show how solar is becoming a game changer in the fight against climate change. World Economic Forum (16 May). https://www.weforum.org/agenda/2023/05/4-charts-solar-energy-fight-climate-change (accessed 8 November 2023).

28. NYSE. (n.d.). The history of NYSE. https://www.nyse.com/history-of-nyse (accessed 1 January 2024).

29. Worldometer. (2023). World population by year. https://www.worldometers.info/world-population/world-population-by-year; Statista. Historical carbon dioxide emissions from global fossil fuel combustion and industrial processes in selected years from 1750 to 2022. https://www.statista.com/statistics/264699/worldwide-co2-emissions (accessed 12 November 2023); Statista. (2023). Average carbon dioxide emissions worldwide per capita. https://www.statista.com/statistics/268753/co2-emissions-per-capita-worldwide-since-1990 (accessed 27 January 2024).

30. Stainforth, T., and Pepinster, S. (2022). CO_2 emissions need to be reduced twice as fast as the rate they have gone up since 1990. Institute European Environmental Policy blog (19 October). https://ieep.eu/news/co2-emissions-need-to-be-reduced-twice-as-fast-as-the-rate-they-have-gone-up-since-1990 (accessed 12 November 2023).

31. Teffer, P. (2015). Norway bans pension fund from coal investment. EUobserver (5 June). https://euobserver.com/green-economy/128976 (accessed 7 November 2023).

32. ABP. (2021). ABP stops investing in fossil fuel producers (press release 26 October). https://www.abp.nl/content/dam/abp/nl/documents/Press%20Release%20Fossil_EN.pdf (accessed 7 November 2023).

33. Australia Retirement Trust. (2023). Australian Retirement Trust targets 43% emission intensity reduction by 2030 across specified asset classes with launch of its Net Zero 2050 Roadmap. Press release (22 September). https://www.australianretirementtrust.com.au/newsroom/art-net-zero-roadmap (accessed 8 November 2023).

34. Eckhouse, B. (2016). Johnson & Johnson buying 100 megawatts of Texas wind power. Bloomberg (16 September). https://www.bloomberg.com/news/articles/2016-09-16/johnson-johnson-buying-100-megawatts-of-texas-wind-power#xj4y7vzkgof (accessed 9 November 2023).

35. Copernicus Climate Change Service. 2023 on track to become the warmest year after record October. https://climate.copernicus.eu/2023-track-become-warmest-year-after-record-october (accessed 12 November 2023).

36. da Victoria Lobo. What will it be: ESG or SOS? Swiss Re blog (13 July). https://www.swissre.com/risk-knowledge/risk-perspectives-blog/esg-or-sos-climate-risk.html#:~:text=According%20to%20Swiss%20Re%20Institute,slow%20to%20embrace%20the%20SDGs%3F (accessed 12 November 2023).

37. Stainforth, T., and Pepinster, S. (2022). CO2 emissions need to be reduced twice as fast as the rate they have gone up since 1990. Institute European Environmental Policy blog (19 October 2022). https://ieep.eu/news/co2-emissions-need-to-be-reduced-twice-as-fast-as-the-rate-they-have-gone-up-since-1990 (accessed 12 November 2023).

Chapter 2

1. Climate Central. (2023). The hottest 12-month stretch in recorded history (9 November). https://assets.ctfassets.net/cxgxgstp8r5d/3Ol753Qyg KfVTuCC28qgij/b97aacad87ca66289e06e2176b7af567/-Climate_Central_report-_The_hottest_12-month_stretch_in_recorded_history__Nov_2022_to_Oct_2023_.pdf (accessed 19 November 2023).

2. UK Office of National Statistics. (2023). Climate change insights, families and households, UK: August 2023 (11 August). https://www.ons.gov.uk/economy/environmentalaccounts/articles/climatechangeinsightsuk/august2023 (accessed 9 November 2023).

3. USGS. (n.d.). What is the difference between global warming and climate change? https://www.usgs.gov/faqs/what-difference-between-global-warming-and-climate-change (accessed 19 November 2023).

4. US Energy Information Agency. (2023). Energy and the environment explained (22 August). https://www.eia.gov/energyexplained/energy-and-the-environment/where-greenhouse-gases-come-from.php (accessed 11 November 2023).

5. Ibid.

6. Global Carbon Project. (2022). Global carbon budget 2022 (11 November 2022). https://globalcarbonbudget.org/wp-content/uploads/GCP_CarbonBudget_2022_slides_v1.0.pdf (accessed 15 November 2023).

7. Persefoni. (2023). ESG terms you need to know. https://www.persefoni.com/learn/top-esg-terms (accessed 1 December 2023).

8. Persefoni. (2023). Carbon neutral versus net zero. https://www.persefoni.com/learn/carbon-neutral-vs-net-zero (accessed 25 October 2023).

9. UKRI. (2021). A brief history of climate change discoveries. https://www.discover.ukri.org/a-brief-history-of-climate-change-discoveries/index.html (accessed 12 November 2023).

10. Ibid.

11. US EPA. (2023). Summary of clean air act. https://www.epa.gov/laws-regulations/summary-clean-air-act (accessed 12 November 2023).

12. Ibid.

13. UN Women. (n.d.). United Nations framework convention on climate change. https://www.unwomen.org/en/how-we-work/intergovernmental-support/climate-change-and-the-environment/united-nations-framework-convention-on-climate-change#:~:text=The%20United%20Nations%20Framework%20Convention,Agreement%20build%20on%20the%20Convention (accessed 20 November 2023).

14. Climate Science 2030. (n.d.). https://climatescience2030.com (accessed 22 November 2023).

15. United Nations. (1992). United Nations Conference on Environment and Development, Rio de Janeiro, Brazil (3–14 June). https://www.un.org/en/conferences/environment/rio1992 (accessed 1 November 2023).

16. Maizland, L. (2023). Global climate agreements: Success and failures. Council on Foreign Relations (5 December). https://www.cfr.org/backgrounder/paris-global-climate-change-agreements (accessed 12 March 2024).

17. Ibid.

18. US Global Change Research Program. (2023). Fifth national climate assessment. https://nca2023.globalchange.gov; Science-Based Targets initiative.

(2023). Lead the way to a low-carbon future. https://sciencebasedtargets.org/how-it-works (accessed 18 November 2023).

19. US Geological Survey. (n.d.). How much carbon dioxide does the United States and the world emit each year from energy sources? https://www.usgs.gov/faqs/how-much-carbon-dioxide-does-united-states-and-world-emit-each-year-energy-sources (accessed 13 November 2023).

20. Conlen, M. (2021). How much carbon dioxide are we emitting? NASA Global Climate Change (15 July). https://climate.nasa.gov/news/3020/how-much-carbon-dioxide-are-we-emitting (accessed 13 November 2023).

21. Auffhammer, M. (2022). Damage per ton of CO2 costs $185, not the official $51. Energypost.eu (7 October). https://energypost.eu/new-u-s-study-damage-per-ton-of-co2-costs-185-not-the-official-51 (accessed 13 November 2023).

22. Global Carbon Project. (2023). Fossil CO_2 emissions at record high in 2023 (4 December). https://globalcarbonbudget.org/fossil-co2-emissions-at-record-high-in-2023 (accessed 5 March 2024).

23. Hansen, J. E., Sato, M., Simmons, L., et al. (2023). Global warming in the pipeline. *Oxford Open Climate Change*, 3 (1), kgad008. https://academic.oup.com/oocc/article/3/1/kgad008/7335889?login=false (accessed 14 November 2023).

Chapter 3

1. UN Intergovernmental Panel on Climate Change. (n.d.). 2.3.2 Stakeholder involvement. https://archive.ipcc.ch/publications_and_data/ar4/wg2/en/ch2s2-3-2.html (accessed 14 November 2023).

2. UN Sustainable Development Goals. (2023). Goal 13: Take urgent action to combat climate and its impacts. https://www.un.org/sustainabledevelopment/climate-change/ (accessed 16 November 2023).

3. European Council. (n.d.). Climate change: What the EU is doing. https://www.consilium.europa.eu/en/policies/climate-change/#2030 (accessed 16 November 2023).

4. Amadeo, K. (2022). Pigouvian taxes: Their pros and cons, and examples. The Balance (2 January). https://www.thebalancemoney.com/pigouvian-tax-definition-and-examples-4157479; FCC Aviation. French noise tax. https://www.fccaviation.com/regulation/france/noise-tax (accessed 23 November 2023).

5. Jahan, S., and Mahmud, A. What is capitalism? International Monetary Fund. https://www.imf.org/en/Publications/fandd/issues/Series/Back-to-Basics/Capitalism (accessed 23 November 2023).

6. Friedman, M. (1970). A Friedman doctrine—The social responsibility of business is to increase its profits. *New York Times* (13 September). https://www.nytimes.com/1970/09/13/archives/a-friedman-doctrine-the-social-responsibility-of-business-is-to.html (accessed 12 November 2023).

7. Government of Canada. (2023). Canada's record-breaking wildfires in 2023: A fiery wake-up call. https://natural-resources.canada.ca/simply-science/canadas-record-breaking-wildfires-2023-fiery-wake-call/25303 (accessed 21 November 2023).

8. Artsy, A. (2023). A climate scientist on how to recognize the new climate change denial. Vox (22 September). https://www.vox.com/climate/23885799/climate-change-denial-fossil-fuel-companies-exxon-mobil (accessed 12 November 2023).

9. Copley, M. (2023). Exxon minimized climate change internally after conceding that fossil fuels cause it. NPR (15 September). https://www.npr.org/2023/09/14/1199570023/exxon-climate-change-fossil-fuels-global-warming-oil-gas (accessed 16 November 2023).

10. Wamsley, L. (2019). Exxon wins New York climate change fraud case. NPR (10 December). https://www.npr.org/2019/12/10/780317799/exxon-wins-new-york-climate-change-case (accessed 12 November 2023).

11. European Coalition for Corporate Justice. (2021). Landmark ruling: Shell ordered to slash CO_2 emissions throughout its global value chain (28 May). https://corporatejustice.org/news/landmark-ruling-shell-ordered-to-slash-co2-emissions-throughout-its-global-value-chain (accessed 12 November 2023).

12. Persefoni. (2023). What is greenwashing and how can businesses avoid it? https://www.persefoni.com/learn/what-is-greenwashing (accessed 10 November 2023).

13. Fair, L. (2022). $5.5 million total FTC settlements with Kohls and Walmart challenge bamboo and eco-claims shed light on penalty, eco-enforcement. FTC blog (8 April). https://www.ftc.gov/business-guidance/blog/2022/04/55-million-total-ftc-settlements-kohls-and-walmart-challenge-bamboo-and-eco-claims-shed-light (accessed 10 November 2023).

14. US DOJ Office of Public Affairs. (2018). Former CEO Volkswagen AG charged with conspiracy and wire fraud in diesel emissions scandal. Press release (3 May). https://www.justice.gov/opa/pr/former-ceo-volkswagen-ag-charged-conspiracy-and-wire-fraud-diesel-emissions-scandal (accessed 14 November 2023).

15. Moneer, Z. (2022). Greenwashing in a time of global warming. Middle East Institute (13 December 2022). https://www.mei.edu/publications/greenwashing-time-global-warming (accessed 22 November 2023).

16. Sabin Center for Climate Change Law. (2020). ASA ruling on Ryanair Ltd. t/a Ryanair Ltd. (5 February). https://climatecasechart.com/non-us-case/asa-ruling-on-ryanair-ltd-t-a-ryanair-ltd (accessed 15 November 2023).

17. Transport & Environment. (2022). Europe's largest airlines claim net zero future whilst lobbying to weaken EU's climate laws. Press release (7 April). https://www.transportenvironment.org/discover/europes-largest-airlines-claim-net-zero-future-whilst-lobbying-to-weaken-eus-climate-laws (accessed 4 December 2023).

18. PwC Global. (2022). Global investor survey 2022. https://www.pwc.com/gx/en/issues/esg/global-investor-survey-2022.html (accessed 22 October 2023). Adapted and reprinted with permission from "PwC's Global Investor Survey 2022" © 2022 PwC. All rights reserved. PwC refers to the PwC network and/or one or more of its member firms, each of which is a separate legal entity. Please see www.pwc.com/structure for further details. [Translation from the original English text as published by PwC arranged by John Wiley & Sons, Inc. (WILEY).]

19. Stewart, N. (2023). Future of the SASB Standards: What you need to know for 2023 disclosure. SASB Standards blog (19 January 2023). https://sasb.org/blog/future-of-the-sasb-standards-what-you-need-to-know-for-2023-reporting; ISSB. (2023). ISSB issues inaugural global sustainability disclosure standards. IFRS (26 June 2023). https://www.ifrs.org/news-and-events/news/2023/06/issb-issues-ifrs-s1-ifrs-s2/ (accessed 10 November 2023).

20. Ibid.

21. Crenshaw, C. (2022). Statement on the Enhancement and Standardization of Climate-Related Disclosures for Investors. FTC (21 March 2022). https://www.sec.gov/news/statement/crenshaw-climate-statement-032122 (accessed 1 November 2023).

22. US FTC. (2012). FTC issues revised green guides (1 October). https://www.ftc.gov/news-events/news/press-releases/2012/10/ftc-issues-revised-green-guides (accessed 10 November 2023).

23. European Commission. (2023). Implementing and delegated acts—SFDR (17 February). https://finance.ec.europa.eu/regulation-and-supervision/financial-services-legislation/implementing-and-delegated-acts/sustainable-finance-disclosures-regulation_en (accessed 10 November 2023).

24. Think Tank, European Parliament. (2023). Green claims directive: Protecting consumers from greenwashing. Briefing (10 May). https://www.europarl.europa.eu/thinktank/en/document/EPRS_BRI(2023)753958 (accessed 10 November 2023).

25. European Commission. (2021) Climate and resilience law. https://commission.europa.eu/projects/climate-and-resilience-law_en (accessed 10 November 2023).

26. European Securities and Markets Authority. (2022). Sustainable finance roadmap 2022–2024 (10 February). https://www.esma.europa.eu/sites/default/files/library/esma30-379-1051_sustainable_finance_roadmap.pdf (accessed 10 November 2023).

27. US Energy Information Administration (2022). Europe is a key destination for Russia's energy exports. Today in energy (20 December) https://www.eia.gov/todayinenergy/detail.php?id=55021 (accessed 10 November 2023).

28. Ibid.

29. Persefoni. (2023). FERF sustainability talent report finds finance leaders focusing on talent as sustainability requirements grow. Press release (13 November). https://www.persefoni.com/insight/ferf-sustainability-talent-report-finds-finance-leaders-focusing-on-talent-as-sustainability-requirements-grow (accessed 1 December 2023).

30. SEC. (2024). Statement on final rules regarding mandatory climate disclosures (6 March). https://www.sec.gov/news/statement/gensler-statement-mandatory-climate-risk-disclosures-030624 (accessed 7 March 2024).

Chapter 4

1. Rivera, A., Movalia, S., Rutkowski, E., Rangel, Y., Pitt, H., and Larsen, K. (2023). Global greenhouse gas emissions 190-2021 and preliminary 2022 estimates. Rhodium Group (19 September). https://rhg.com/research/global-greenhouse-gas-emissions-2022 (accessed 12 November 2023).

2. US Energy Information Administration. (2022). Fossil fuel sources accounted for 79% of U.S. consumption of primary energy in 2021. Today in Energy (1 July). https://www.eia.gov/todayinenergy/detail.php?id=52959 (accessed 17 November 2023).

3. Farrell, J. (2019). Senate Dems Special Committee on the Climate Crisis hearing. YouTube video. https://www.youtube.com/watch?v=AxaICTiNKvY (accessed 18 November 2023).

4. Black, J. (1978). Letter to F. G. Turpin, Exxon Research and Engineering Company, vice president (6 June). Obtained by Inside Climate News. https://insideclimatenews.org/wp-content/uploads/2015/09/James-Black-1977-Presentation.pdf (accessed 14 December 2023).

5. Center for International Environmental Law. (n.d.). BP acknowledged risk of fossil fuels in 1990. Press release. https://www.ciel.org/news/bp-acknowledged-climate-risk-of-fossil-fuels-in-1990 (accessed 18 November 2023).

6. Changerism. (2020). Dirty pearls: Exposing Shell's hidden legacy of climate change accountability, 1970–1990. https://changerism.com/portfolio/dirty-pearls-exposing-shells-hidden-legacy-of-climate-change-accountability-1970-1990/ (accessed 18 November 2023).

7. Haq, A. (2016). Peabody Coal's unprecedented support for climate denial. NRDC blog (17 June). https://www.nrdc.org/bio/aliya-haq/peabody-coals-unprecedented-support-climate-denial#:~:text=This%20week%2C%20researchers%20confirmed%20that,and%20the%20Clean%20Power%20Plan (accessed 18 November 2023).
8. ExxonMobil. (2023). ExxonMobil completes acquisition of Denbury. Press release (2 November). https://corporate.exxonmobil.com/news/news-releases/2023/1102_exxonmobil-completes-acquisition-of-denbury (accessed 18 November 2023).
9. OK Energy Today. (2023). Exxon to begin lithium production after deal with OKC energy firm (13 November). https://www.okenergytoday.com/2023/11/114948/ (accessed 18 November 2023).
10. Grancio, J. (2023) Engine No. 1 CEO on Exxon's lithium investments. YouTube video (2023). https://www.youtube.com/watch?v=PIBY_Wh7-74 (accessed 8 November, 2023).
11. BP. Our transformation. https://www.bp.com/en_us/united-states/home/who-we-are/our-transformation.html; BP. Getting to net zero climate advocacy in the U.S. https://www.bp.com/en_us/united-states/home/who-we-are/advocating-for-net-zero-in-the-us.html (accessed 8 November 2023).
12. Jordans, F. (2023). More companies setting net-zero climate targets, but few have credible plans, report says. AP News (11 June). https://apnews.com/article/climate-change-net-zero-report-7b791ade530432caea4ef3a4ffe0fb4e; Net Zero Tracker (2023). Net Zero Stocktake 2023. https://zerotracker.net/analysis/net-zero-stocktake-2023 (accessed 22 November 2023).
13. Irving, T. (2020). Electric vehicles can fight climate change but they're not silver bullet: U of T study. *University of Toronto News* (29 September). https://www.utoronto.ca/news/electric-vehicles-can-fight-climate-change-they-re-not-silver-bullet-u-t-study (accessed 18 November 2023).
14. Kim, A. (2022). Lithium: Not as clean as we thought. Climate360 News (14 January). https://climate360news.lmu.edu/lithium-not-as-clean-as-we-thought (accessed 18 November 2023).
15. US Energy Information Administration. (2022). Fossil fuel sources accounted for 79% of U.S. consumption of primary energy in 2021. Today in Energy (1 July). https://www.eia.gov/todayinenergy/detail.php?id=52959 (accessed 17 November 2023).
16. Black, Letter to F. G. Turpin.
17. Jordans, More companies setting net-zero climate targets.

Chapter 5

1. Corbett, M. (Federal Reserve Bank of Boston). Oil shock of 1973–74. https://www.federalreservehistory.org/essays/oil-shock-of-1973-74 (accessed 2 December 2023).

2. Reuters. (2023). Why did OPEC cut oil production? Key reasons explained (3 April). https://www.reuters.com/business/energy/why-is-opec-cutting-oil-output-2023-04-03 (accessed 2 December 2023).

3. US Energy Information Administration. What drives crude oil prices: Supply OPEC. https://www.eia.gov/finance/markets/crudeoil/supply-opec.php (accessed 2 December 2023).

4. OPEC. Brief history. https://www.opec.org/opec_web/en/about_us/24.htm (accessed 2 December 2023).

5. Norges Bank Investment Management. (2023). Sharpened expectations on climate (15 September). https://www.nbim.no/en/the-fund/news-list/2023/sharpened-expectations-on-climate (accessed 29 November 2023).

6. Smith, C. (2022). Oxford Sustainable Finance Summit 2022/Session VI Stewardship and engagement (4 August). https://www.youtube.com/watch?v=1OCMUOVLXwI (accessed 29 November 2023).

7. Energyworld.com/Reuters. (2023). Australia's biggest pension funds raise investment in fossil fuels, activist group says (8 May). https://energy.economictimes.indiatimes.com/news/oil-and-gas/australias-biggest-pension-funds-raise-investment-in-fossil-fuels-activist-group-says/100065713 (accessed 29 November 2023).

8. Australian Retirement Trust. Sustainable investing. https://www.australianretirementtrust.com.au/investments/how-we-invest/responsible-investing (accessed 29 November 2023).

9. Buis, A. (2022). Steamy relationships: How atmospheric water vapor amplifies Earth's greenhouse effect. NASA's Jet Propulsion Laboratory (8 February). https://climate.nasa.gov/explore/ask-nasa-climate/3143/steamy-relationships-how-atmospheric-water-vapor-amplifies-earths-greenhouse-effect/#:~:text=For%20every%20degree%20Celsius%20that,to%20the%20laws%20of%20thermodynamics.&text=Some%20people%20mistakenly%20believe%20water,driver%20of%20Earth's%20current%20warming (accessed 5 January 2024).

10. Ray, C. (2019). Rejecting reality: Kiribati's shifting climate change policies. Climate Security in Oceania, University of Texas–Austin (31 December). https://sites.utexas.edu/climatesecurity/2019/12/31/kiribati-policy-shift; Human Rights Watch. (2018). Interview: Climate change and the disappearing islands of Kiribati (15 June). https://www.hrw.org/

news/2018/06/15/interview-climate-change-and-disappearing-islands-kiribati?gad_source=1&gclid=CjwKCAiAx_GqBhBQEiwAlDNAZn bySTotgtHSK7ayBTBa2AAIeMLGbSIGwP1BCp6yf3F53bOyq47yex oCdKMQAvD_BwE; Duff, M. (2023). Which islands will become uninhabitable due to climate change first? Live Science (12 November). https://www.livescience.com/planet-earth/climate-change/which-islands-will-become-uninhabitable-due-to-climate-change-first#:~:text= About%20a%20million%20people%20live,will%20result%20from%20 climate%20change (accessed 29 November 2023).

11. Boyle, L. (2022). How global warming is threatening California wine. *Independent* (19 June). https://www.independent.co.uk/climate-change/ news/california-wine-blobal-warming-wildfire-b2104209.html (accessed 29 November 2023).

12. O'Hara, C., Ranches, J. Roche, L., Schohr, T., Busch, R., and Maier, G. (2021). Impacts from wildfires on livestock health and production, producer perspectives. *NIH National Library of Medicine* (11 November). https://www.ncbi.nlm.nih.gov/pmc/articles/PMC8614491 (accessed 28 November 2023).

13. Tong, A. (2023). Address to General Assembly of the United Nations (26 September). https://www.un.org/en/ga/69/meetings/gadebate/26sep/ kiribati.shtml (accessed 23 November 2023).

14. Forrester. (2023). Predictions 2024. https://go.forrester.com/wp-content/ uploads/2023/10/Forrester-Predictions-2024.pdf?_gl=1*mtdybx*_ga*Nz czNzUzODIxLjE3MDE3MjY3Njg.*_ga_PMXYWTHPVN*MTcwMTcy Njc2Ny4xLjEuMTcw (accessed 24 November 2023).

15. Ibid.

16. US Commodity Futures Trading Corporation Climate-Related Market Risk Subcommittee. (2020). Managing Climate Risk in the U.S. Financial System. https://www.cftc.gov/sites/default/files/2020-09/9-9-20%20 Report%20of%20the%20Subcommittee%20on%20Climate-Related%20Market%20Risk%20-%20Managing%20Climate%20 Risk%20in%20the%20U.S.%20Financial%20System%20for%20 posting.pdf (accessed 29 November 2023).

17. Ganu, S., and Wong, J. (2021). Climate action no longer a moral question but a fiduciary duty for boards. WTW (18 October). https://www .wtwco.com/en-us/insights/2021/10/climate-action-no-longer-a-moral-question-but-a-fiduciary-duty-for-boards (accessed 19 November 2023).

18. Clark, L. (2023). Climate activists end 2023 with major court wins. *ClimateWire* (22 December). https://www.eenews.net/articles/climate-activists-end-2023-with-major-court-wins (accessed 12 March 2024).

19. US EPA. (n.d.). Sulfur hexafluoride basics. https://www.epa.gov/eps-partnership/sulfur-hexafluoride-sf6-basics (accessed 29 November 2023).

20. General Electric. Sustainability/g3 bringing novel solutions to the market (2023). https://www.ge.com/renewableenergy/sustainability (accessed 29 November 2023).

21. Cairns, R. (2022). This giant water battery under the Alps could be a gamechanger for renewable energy in Europe. CNN (1 August). https://edition.cnn.com/2022/08/01/world/water-battery-switzerland-renewable-energy-climate-scn-hnk-spc-intl/index.html (accessed 27 November 2023).

22. IATA. Developing sustainable aviation fuel. https://www.iata.org/en/programs/environment/sustainable-aviation-fuels (accessed 29 November 2023).

23. US Department of Energy. Sustainable airline fuel. Alternative Fuels Data Center. https://afdc.energy.gov/fuels/sustainable_aviation_fuel.html (accessed 29 November 2023).

24. General Dynamics. (2023). Gulfstream completes world's first trans-Atlantic flight on 100% sustainable aviation fuel. PR Newswire (20 November). https://www.prnewswire.com/news-releases/gulfstream-completes-worlds-first-trans-atlantic-flight-on-100-sustainable-aviation-fuel-301993029.html (accessed 29 November 2023).

25. IATA. (2023). Chart of the Week (1 September). https://www.iata.org/en/iata-repository/publications/economic-reports/sustainable-aviation-fuel-output-increases-but-volumes-still-low (accessed 28 November 2023).

26. Clarkson, N. (2023). Flight 100: Virgin Atlantic flies its first 100% sustainable aviation fuel flight. Press release (28 November). https://www.virgin.com/about-virgin/latest/flight100-virgin-atlantic-flies-its-first-100-sustainable-aviation-fuel (accessed 29 November 2023).

27. World Meteorological Organizations. (2020). The value of surface-based meteorological observation data: Costs and benefits of the Global Basic Observing Network. SOFF Series No. 1. https://library.wmo.int/viewer/57167?medianame=P1_The_value_of_Surface_Based_Meteorological_Observation_Data_Costs_and_benefits_of_the_Global_Basic_Observing_Network_#page=2&viewer=picture&o=bookmark&n=0&q= (accessed 20 November 2023).

28. Ask MIT Climate. (2023). Will climate change make weather forecasting less accurate? (30 January). https://climate.mit.edu/ask-mit/will-climate-change-make-weather-forecasting-less-accurate (accessed 12 November 2023).

29. Garthwaite, J. (2021). Climate of chaos: Stanford researchers show why heat may make weather less predictable. Stanford News (14 December).

https://news.stanford.edu/2021/12/14/warming-makes-weather-less-predictable (accessed 12 November 2023).

30. Hoover CS. (2023) Services. https://hooversolutions.com/services (accessed 9 November 2023).

31. Our Next Energy. (2023). Our Next Energy (ONE) raises $300 million in series B equity, Valuing company at over $1 billion. Press release (1 February). https://www.riverstonellc.com/media/1337/our-next-energy-series-b-final.pdf (accessed 9 November 2023).

32. HERE. (2023). Lithium-ion batteries vs. lithium-iron-phosphate batteries: Which is better? *HERE360 News* (31 July). https://www.here.com/learn/blog/lithium-ion-vs-lithium-iron-phosphate (accessed 12 November 2023).

33. Onyx. (2023) Preparation of hydrogen production project in Rotterdam. https://www.onyx-power.com/en/news-and-press/preparation-of-hydrogen-production-project-in-rotterdam/; Port of Rotterdam. (2023). Onyx plans to build plant for blue hydrogen. Press release (7 April). https://www.portofrotterdam.com/en/news-and-press-releases/onyx-plans-to-build-plant-for-blue-hydrogen (accessed 12 November 2023).

Chapter 6

1. Rotman, M. (n.d.). Cuyahoga River fire: The blaze that started a national discussion. Cleveland Historical. https://clevelandhistorical.org/items/show/63 (accessed 16 January 2024).

2. Amazon Staff. (2023). Everything you need to know about The Climate Pledge. Amazon (29 September). https://www.aboutamazon.com/news/sustainability/what-is-the-climate-pledge (accessed 11 March 2024).

3. Silverstein, K. (2024). Panama's high court prizes ecosystems over copper mining: The impact. *Forbes* (15 January). https://www.forbes.com/sites/kensilverstein/2024/01/15/panamas-high-court-prizes-ecosystems-over-copper-mining-the-impact/?sh=3bb3bd1cf5a3 (accessed 16 January 2024).

4. Kushida, K. (2024). The Silicon Valley model and technological model in context. Carnegie Endowment for International Peace (9 January). https://carnegieendowment.org/2024/01/09/silicon-valley-model-and-technological-trajectories-in-context-pub-91347 (accessed 25 January 2024).

5. Kiniulis, M. (2023). Entrepreneur statistics: Industry insights. Markinblog (19 October). https://www.markinblog.com/entrepreneur-statistics/#fn-10037-18 (accessed 19 January 2024).

6. Unilever. (2020). Unilever sets out new actions to fight climate change, and protect and regenerate nature, to preserve resources for future generations. Press release (15 June). https://www.unilever.com/news/press-and-media/press-releases/2020/unilever-sets-out-new-actions-to-fight-climate-change-and-protect-and-regenerate-nature-to-preserve-resources-for-future-generations (accessed 12 November 2023).

7. Planet Tracker. (2023). Unilever on a 2°C trajectory by 2030 with key challenges linked to Scope 3 emissions (18 May). https://planet-tracker.org/unilever-on-a-2c-trajectory-by-2030-with-key-challenges-linked-to-scope-3-emissions (accessed 20 November 2023).

8. The Climate Pledge. (2019). Leading the charge on climate change. Amazon. https://www.theclimatepledge.com/us/en/History; Amazon Sustainability (2023). Driving climate solutions. https://sustainability.aboutamazon.com/climate-solutions (accessed 25 November 2023).

9. Schroders. (2023). Schroders institutional investor study 2023: Investors target sustainability and private assets amid energy transition opportunities as inflation concerns remain (3 October). https://www.schroders.com/en/global/individual/media-centre/schroders-institutional-investor-study-2023-investors-target-sustainability-and-private-assets-amid-energy-transition-opportunities-as-inflation-concerns-remain (accessed 11 November 2023).

10. Schwartzkopt, F., and Bloomberg. (2023). World's No. 1 ESG fund class ratchets up oil, gas exposure. Rig Zone (13 December). https://www.rigzone.com/news/wire/worlds_no_1_esg_fund_class_ratchets_up_oil_gas_exposure-13-dec-2023-175043-article (accessed 12 November 2023).

11. US Securities and Exchange Commission. (2022). The enhancement and standardization of climate related disclosures for investors. Proposed rule (10 October). https://www.sec.gov/files/rules/proposed/2022/33-11042.pdf (accessed 12 November 2023).

12. Carbon Disclosure Project. (2023). Record 23,000+ companies disclose environmental impact through CDP, with urgency for action clear in wake of unprecedented global temperatures. CDP (18 October). https://www.cdp.net/en/articles/companies/record-23-000-companies-disclose-environmental-impact-through-cdp-with-urgency-for-action-clear-in-wake-of-unprecedented-global-temperatures (accessed 5 December 2023).

13. Shum, L ., Jeong, W., and Chen, K. (2022). Climate adaptation: The $2 trillion market the private sector cannot ignore. World Economic Forum (1 November). https://www.weforum.org/agenda/2022/11/climate-change-climate-adaptation-private-sector (accessed 4 December 2023).

14. United Nations Climate Change. (2023). COP28 agreement signals "beginning of the end" of the fossil fuel era climate. Press release (13 December). https://unfccc.int/news/cop28-agreement-signals-beginning-of-the-end-of-the-fossil-fuel-era; AFP. (2023). Cause for optimism: World reacts to COP28 climate deal. *Barron's* (13 December). https://www.barrons.com/news/cause-for-optimism-world-reacts-to-cop28-climate-deal-9a7fadbc (accessed 22 December 2023).

15. UN Environment Programme. (2023). Broken record: Temperatures hit new highs, yet world fails to cut emissions (again). https://wedocs.unep.org/bitstream/handle/20.500.11822/43922/EGR2023.pdf?sequence=3&isAllowed=y; United Nations Climate Action. (n.d.). Is there a global effort to reach net zero? https://www.un.org/en/climatechange/net-zero-coalition#:~:text=Yes%2C%20a%20growing%20coalition%20of,about%2088%25%20of%20global%20emissions (accessed 20 November 2023).

16. Ibid.

17. Net Zero Tracker. (2023). Net zero stocktake 2023 (June). https://zerotracker.net/analysis/net-zero-stocktake-2023 (accessed 20 November 2023).

18. Chancel, L. (2022). World inequality report. World Inequality Lab. https://wir2022.wid.world/www-site/uploads/2022/03/0098-21_WIL_RIM_RAPPORT_A4.pdf (accessed 8 December 2023).

19. Myers, J. (2021). These charts show the growing income inequality between the world's richest and poorest. World Economic Forum (10 December). https://www.weforum.org/agenda/2021/12/global-income-inequality-gap-report-rich-poor (accessed 19 January 2024).

20. UN Environment Programme, Broken record: Temperatures hit new highs, yet world fails to cut emissions (again).

21. Deloitte. (2022). Emerging trends for ESG governance for 2023. https://www2.deloitte.com/us/en/pages/center-for-board-effectiveness/articles/emerging-trends-in-esg-governance-for-2023.html (accessed 12 November 2023).

Chapter 7

1. Market Insights Report. (2023). Traditional capital raising: Market & data analysis. Statista. https://www.statista.com/study/137408/traditional-capital-raising-report (accessed 20 January 2024).

2. BBVA. (2023). BBVA brings its investment in decarbonization funds to €108 million. Press release (8 November). https://www.bbva.com/en/sustainability/bbva-brings-its-investment-in-decarbonization-funds-to-e108-million (accessed 23 November 2023).

3. US Environmental Protection Agency. (2019). Repeal of the clean power plan. EPA Fact Sheet (19 June). https://www.epa.gov/sites/default/files/2019-06/documents/cpp_repeal_fact_sheet_6.18.19_final.pdf (accessed 20 January 2024).

4. Hargreaves, S. (2012). Obama's alternative energy bankruptcies. CNN Business (22 October). https://money.cnn.com/2012/10/22/news/economy/obama-energy-bankruptcies/index.html (accessed 20 January 2024).

5. Bowers, D. (2011). The loan program that helped Solyndra "was a program that was supported by President Bush." PolitiFact (17 November). https://www.politifact.com/factchecks/2011/nov/17/david-plouffe/solyndra-loan-george-w-bush-david-plouffe (20 January 2024).

6. Hargreaves, Obama's alternative energy bankruptcies.

7. Gaddy, B., Sivaram, V., and O'Sullivan, F. (2016). Venture capital and cleantech: The wrong model for clean energy innovation. MIT Energy Initiative (July). https://energy.mit.edu/wp-content/uploads/2016/07/MITEI-WP-2016-06.pdf (accessed 25 January 2024).

8. Kanoff, C., Chandaria, K., Mohla, K., et al. (2023). From clean tech 1.0 to climate tech 2.0: A new era of investment opportunities. B Capital (17 January). https://b.capital/from-clean-tech-1-0-to-climate-tech-2-0-a-new-era-of-investment-opportunities/#section2 (accessed 25 January 2024).

9. Ibid.

Chapter 8

1. World Bank. (2021). Climate change governance (6 December). https://www.worldbank.org/en/news/feature/2021/12/06/climate-change-governance (accessed 12 November 2023).

2. US Department of Energy. (2022). Biden-Harris administration announces $3.7 billion to kickstart America's carbon dioxide removal industry. Press release (13 December). https://www.energy.gov/articles/biden-harris-administration-announces-37-billion-kick-start-americas-carbon-dioxide (accessed 16 November 2023).

3. US Department of Energy. (2023). Biden-Harris administration announces $3.5 billion to strengthen domestic battery manufacturing. Press release (15 November). https://www.energy.gov/articles/biden-harris-administration-announces-35-billion-strengthen-domestic-battery-manufacturing (accessed 5 December 2023).

4. Black, S., Liu, A.A., Parry, I. W. H., and Vernon, N. (2023). IMF fossil fuel subsidies data: 2023 update. International Monetary Fund (24 August).

https://www.imf.org/en/Publications/WP/Issues/2023/08/22/IMF-Fossil-Fuel-Subsidies-Data-2023-Update-537281 (accessed 22 November 2023).

5. Jones, H. (2023). UK adopts international climate disclosures to bolster global investor appeal. Reuters (2 August). https://www.reuters.com/world/uk/uk-adopts-international-climate-disclosures-bolster-global-investor-appeal-2023-08-02 (accessed 1 November 2023).

6. European Council. (2023). Climate change: What the EU is doing (12 November). https://www.consilium.europa.eu/en/policies/climate-change/#2030 (accessed 12 November 2023).

7. IFRS. (2023). General sustainability related disclosures. https://www.ifrs.org/projects/completed-projects/2023/general-sustainability-related-disclosures/#about (accessed 12 November 2023).

8. US Securities and Exchange Commission. (2022). Proposed rule 17 CFR 210, 229, 232, 239, and 249. The enhancement and standardization of climate related disclosures for investors. https://www.sec.gov/files/rules/proposed/2022/33-11042.pdf (accessed 30 November 2023).

9. SEC.GOV. (2024). Fact Sheet: Enhancement and Standardization of Climate-Related Disclosures (6 March). https://www.sec.gov/files/33-11042-fact-sheet.pdf(accessed 3 March 2024).

10. King, B., Gauffney, M., and Rivera, A. (2024). Preliminary U.S. greenhouse gas estimates for 2023. Rhodium Group (10 January). https://rhg.com/research/us-greenhouse-gas-emissions-2023 (accessed 12 January 2024).

11. World Bank, Climate change governance.

12. Ibid.

13. Google. (2023). 24/7 by 2030: Realizing a carbon-free future (September) https://www.gstatic.com/gumdrop/sustainability/247-carbon-free-energy.pdf; Terrell, M. (2023). A first-of-its-kind geothermal project is now operational. Google blog (28 November). https://blog.google/outreach-initiatives/sustainability/google-fervo-geothermal-energy-partnership (accessed 30 November 2023).

14. Project InnerSpace. (2023). Project InnerSpace joins forces with Google to advance geothermal exploration. Press release (13 September). https://www.prweb.com/releases/project-innerspace-joins-forces-with-google-to-advance-geothermal-exploration-301925928.html (accessed 18 November 2023).

15. *Business Wire.* (2023). DOE awards $165M GEODE grant to consortium formed by Project InnerSpace, the Society of Petroleum Engineering International, and Geothermal Rising. Press release (4 May). https://www.businesswire.com/news/home/20230504006061/en/DOE-awards-165M-GEODE-grant-to-consortium-formed-by-Project-

InnerSpace-the-Society-of-Petroleum-Engineering-International-and-Geothermal-Rising (accessed 26 January 2024).

16. Equinor. (2023). Dogger bank. https://doggerbank.com; Frangoul, A. (2023). The world's largest offshore wind farm produces its first power. CNBC (9 October). https://www.cnbc.com/2023/10/09/the-worlds-largest-offshore-wind-farm-produces-its-first-power.html (accessed 22 November 2023).

17. Ibid.

18. Equinor. (2023). We're going for net zero by 2050, but what does that really mean? https://www.equinor.com/sustainability/climate-ambitions (accessed 22 November 2023).

19. US EPA. (2023). What is emissions trading? https://www.epa.gov/emissions-trading-resources/what-emissions-trading (accessed 12 November 2023).

20. EY Americas. (2021). How businesses need to navigate environmental incentives and penalties. (7 September). https://www.ey.com/en_us/tax/how-businesses-need-to-navigate-environmental-incentives-and-penalties (accessed 12 November 2023).

21. US EPA. (2023). How do emissions trading programs work. https://www.epa.gov/emissions-trading-resources/how-do-emissions-trading-programs-work#:~:text=Limit%20on%20Pollution%20Emissions,of%20an%20emissions%20trading%20program (accessed 12 November 2023).

22. Thronsen, M. (2023). Norway celebrates another record-breaking year for electric vehicles. Norsk elbilforening (1 February). https://elbil.no/norway-celebrates-another-record-breaking-year-for-electric-vehicles (accessed 24 November 2023).

23. Gross, S. (2020). Why are fossil fuels so hard to quit? Brookings (June). https://www.brookings.edu/articles/why-are-fossil-fuels-so-hard-to-quit/#:~:text=Instead%2C%20fossil%20fuels%20allowed%20the,processes%2C%20agriculture%2C%20and%20transportation (accessed 23 November 2023).

24. Zipper, D. (2023). Why Norway—the poster child for electric cars—is having second thoughts. Vox (31 October). https://www.vox.com/future-perfect/23939076/norway-electric-vehicle-cars-evs-tesla-oslo (accessed 31 October 2023).

25. FuelEconomy.gov. (2023). Federal tax credits for plug-in electric and fuel cell vehicles purchased in 2023 or after. US Department of Energy Office of Energy Efficiency and Renewable Energy. https://fueleconomy.gov/feg/tax2023.shtml (accessed 10 January 2024).

26. US Internal Revenue Service. (2024). Topic A: Frequently asked questions about the eligibility rules for the new clean vehicle credit. *IRS Fact Sheet*

2023-29 (10 January). https://www.irs.gov/newsroom/topic-a-frequently-asked-questions-about-the-eligibility-rules-for-the-new-clean-vehicle-credit-under-ss30d-effective-jan-1-2023 (accessed 10 January 2024).

27. The Weekly Squeeze. (2023). 2023 guide to U.S. e-bike rebates & tax credits. Juiced Bikes (20 July) https://www.juicedbikes.com/blogs/news/2023-guide-us-ebike-rebates-and-tax-credits (accessed 1 December 2023).

28. Gee, M., Friedrich, J., and Vigna, L. (2020). 4 charts explain greenhouse gas emissions by countries and sectors. World Resources Institute (6 February). https://www.wri.org/insights/4-charts-explain-greenhouse-gas-emissions-countries-and-sectors (accessed 1 December 2023).

29. Scientists for Global Responsibility. (2022). New estimate suggests global military activities responsible for more emissions than Russia. (10 November). https://www.sgr.org.uk/resources/new-estimate-suggests-global-military-activities-responsible-more-emissions-russia (accessed 22 November 2023).

30. Kehrt, S. (2022). We must do our part to mitigate climate change: The military's pollution problem. The War Horse (6 January). https://thewarhorse.org/?s=Neta+C.+Crawford; Kehrt, S. (2022). The U.S. military emits more carbon dioxide into the atmosphere than entire countries like Denmark or Portugal. *Inside Climate News* (18 January). https://insideclimatenews.org/news/18012022/military-carbon-emissions/?gclid=CjwKCAiAvJarBhA1EiwAGgZl0EkVSDb92vGnhG7szGpPqP6ZFrKj0eyj9oFq7uzMA8plx9aXnD2oFhoCDZ8QAvD_BwE (accessed 10 November 2023).

31. Office of the Chief Sustainability Officer. (2023). 100% zero-emission vehicle acquisitions by 2035, including 100% light-duty acquisitions by 2027. Sustainability.gov. https://www.sustainability.gov/federalsustainabilityplan/fleet.html (accessed 22 November 2023).

32. Ibid.

Chapter 9

1. evHub. (2024). Were Teslas the first electric vehicles? https://electricvehiclehub.com.au/information-centre/were-teslas-the-first-electric-vehicles (accessed 21 January 2024).

2. Tesla. (2011). Tesla Motors reports fourth-quarter and full-year 2010 results. Press release (15 February). https://www.tesla.com/blog/tesla-motors-reports-fourth-quarter-and-full-year-2010-results (accessed 21 January 2024).

3. Scaringe, R. (2024). LinkedIn profile. https://www.linkedin.com/in/rj-scaringe-58355716 (accessed 21 January 2024).

4. McIntyre, D. A. (2023). Rivian burns toward the ground. 24/7 Wall St. (24 October). https://247wallst.com/autos/2023/10/03/rivian-burns-toward-the-ground (accessed 21 January 2024).

5. Ohsman, A. (2022). Tesla's long-time partner Panasonic building batter plant in Kansas. *Forbes* (13 July). https://www.forbes.com/sites/alanohnsman/2022/07/13/teslas-long-time-partner-panasonic-building-4-billion-ev-battery-plant-in-kansas/?sh=423549396c51 (accessed 21 January 2024).

6. Ecole Polytechnique Fédérale de Lausanne. (2021). Graphene filter makes carbon capture more efficient and cheaper. EurekAlert (American Association for the Advancement of Science). Press release (25 February). https://www.eurekalert.org/news-releases/852869 (accessed 21 January 2024).

7. US Department of Treasury. Instructions for form 8933: Carbon oxide sequestration credit (December 2023). https://www.irs.gov/site-index-search?search=45Q&field_pup_historical_1=1&field_pup_historical=1 (accessed 5 March 2024).

8. Graphyte Inc. (n.d.). Raising the curtain on carbon casting. https://www.graphyte.com (accessed 23 January 2024).

9. Stiffler, L. (2023). Bill Gates–backed startup can store carbon underground for 1,000 years in plant-based bricks. GeekWire. https://www.graphyte.com/post/bill-gates-backed-startup-can-store-carbon-underground-for-1-000-years-in-plant-based-bricks (accessed 23 January 2024).

10. University of California–Davis. (2023). What is technological carbon sequestration? https://www.ucdavis.edu/climate/definitions/carbon-sequestration/technological (accessed 23 January 2024).

11. Riedl, P., Byrum, Z., Li, S., et al. (2023). 5 things to know about carbon mineralization as a carbon removal strategy. World Resources Institute (22 June). https://www.wri.org/insights/carbon-mineralization-carbon-removal (accessed 22 January 2024).

12. CarbonCure. (n.d.). Concrete that matters. https://www.carboncure.com (accessed 2 December 2023).

13. Congressional Research Service. (2023). Cement: Background and Low-Carbon Production (30 November). https://sgp.fas.org/crs/misc/IF12526.pdf (accessed 10 March 2024).

14. Leung, Y., Guzzafame, M., and Minson, A. (2023). Low carbon design can reduce cement emissions by 40% —here's how to deploy it at scale. World Economic Forum (21 March). https://www.weforum.org/agenda/

2023/03/low.carbon-design-can-almost-halve-cement-emissions-here-s-how-to-deploy-it-at-scale (accessed 2 December 2023).
15. Ibid.

Chapter 10

1. Iceland on the Web. (2023). Geothermal heat. https://www .icelandontheweb.com/articles-on-iceland/nature/geology/geothermal-heat#:~:text=Iceland%20is%20one%20of%20the,Iceland%20holds%20enormous%20geothermal%20resources (accessed 5 December 2023).
2. Focus Taiwan. (2023). Taiwan to soon open 1st geothermal plant powered by volcano. *CNA English News* (5 October). https://focustaiwan.tw/business/202310050016 (accessed 5 December 2023).
3. Ali, U. (2019). The history of the oil and gas industry from 347 AD to today. Offshore Technology (7 March). https://www.offshore-technology .com/comment/history-oil-gas/?cf-view (accessed 17 November 2023).
4. US Energy Information Administration. (n.d.). Natural gas explained. https://www.eia.gov/energyexplained/natural-gas/natural-gas-and-the-environment.php (accessed 23 January 2024).
5. United Nations Environment Programme. (2023). Is natural gas really the bridge fuel the world needs? UN Climate Action (12 January). https://www.unep.org/news-and-stories/story/natural-gas-really-bridge-fuel-world-needs (accessed 23 January 2024).
6. US National Renewable Energy Lab. (2023). Solar energy basics. https://www.nrel.gov/news/video/solar-energy-basics-text.html (accessed 20 November 2023).
7. Ibid.
8. Friedlander, B. (2023). Returning solar panel production to U.S. eases climate change. *Cornell Chronicle* (9 March). https://news.cornell.edu/stories/2023/03/returning-solar-panel-production-us-eases-climate-change (accessed 5 November 2023).
9. Solar Learning Center. (n.d.). Solar panel efficiency: Pick the most efficient solar panels. https://www.solar.com/learn/solar-panel-efficiency (accessed 19 January 2024).
10. NREL. (2022). NREL creates highest efficiency 1-sun solar cell. US Department of Energy National Renewable Energy Laboratory. Press release (18 May). https://www.nrel.gov/news/press/2022/nrel-creates-highest-efficiency-1-sun-solar-cell.html (accessed 19 January 2024).

11. Atasu, A., Duran, S., and Van Wassenhove, L. N. (2021). The dark side of solar power. *Harvard Business Review* (18 June). https://hbr.org/2021/06/the-dark-side-of-solar-power (accessed 20 November 2023).
12. Stella, C. (2019). Unfurling the waste problem caused by wind energy. NPR (10 September). https://www.npr.org/2019/09/10/759376113/unfurling-the-waste-problem-caused-by-wind-energy (accessed 20 November 2023).
13. History of Windmills. (n.d.). History of windmills. http://www.historyofwindmills.com; US Energy Information Administration. (2023). Wind explained. (20 April). https://www.eia.gov/energyexplained/wind/history-of-wind-power.php (accessed 20 November 2023).
14. Reve. (2023). Biggest wind farms in the world (19 August). https://www.evwind.es/2023/08/19/biggest-wind-farms-in-the-world/93575 (accessed 20 November 2023).
15. Renewables.digital. (2023). List of the 3 largest onshore wind farms in the U.S. (19 July). https://renewables.digital/list-of-the-3-largest-onshore-wind-farms-in-the-us-2023 (accessed 20 November 2023).
16. US Department of Energy. (2023). U.S. Department of Energy projects strong growth in U.S. wind power sector. Press release (24 August). https://www.energy.gov/articles/us-department-energy-projects-strong-growth-us-wind-power-sector (accessed 20 November 2023).
17. Associated Press. (2023). In a setback for the wind industry, 2 large offshore projects are canceled in N.J. NPR (1 November). https://www.npr.org/2023/11/01/1209986572/offshore-wind-energy-new-jersey-orsted (accessed 30 November 2023).
18. Reuters. (2023). U.S. gives final nod to Rhode Island's $1.5 billion offshore wind farm (7 December). https://www.reuters.com/world/us/us-gives-final-nod-rhode-islands-15-billion-offshore-wind-farm-2023-12-07 (accessed 9 December 2023).
19. Global Fiberglass Solutions. (n.d.). Global fiberglass solutions pellets. https://globalfiberglass.com/pellets (accessed 20 November 2023).
20. Jaganmohan, M. Leading countries in nuclear energy consumption worldwide in 2022. Statista (9 January 2024). https://www.statista.com/statistics/265539/nuclear-energy-consumption-in-leading-countries/#:~:text=In%202022%2C%20the%20United%20States,up%20China%20and%20France%20combined (accessed 4 March 2024).
21. World Nuclear Association. (2023). Nuclear power in Japan (November). https://world-nuclear.org/information-library/country-profiles/countries-g-n/japan-nuclear-power.aspx (accessed 20 November 2023).
22. Vlasov, A. (2023). Thorium's long-term potential in nuclear energy: New IAEA analysis. International Atomic Energy Agency (13 March).

https://www.iaea.org/newscenter/news/thoriums-long-term-potential-in-nuclear-energy-new-iaea-analysis#:~:text=In%20August%202021%2C%20China%20announced,few%20years%20will%20undergo%20testing (accessed 20 November 2023).

23. Clifford, C. (2022). Bill Gates–backed nuclear demonstration project in Wyoming delayed because Russia was the only fuel source. CNBC (19 December). https://www.cnbc.com/2022/12/16/bill-gates-backed-nuclear-demonstration-delayed-by-at-least-2-years.html accessed 20 November 2023).

24. Terra Power. (2023). TerraPower and Uranium Energy Corp. announce MOU to collaborate on domestic uranium fuel supply for the Natrium reactor. Press release (30 November). https://www.terrapower.com/terrapower-and-uranium-energy-corp-announce-mou-to-collaborate-on-domestic-uranium-fuel-supply-for-the-natrium-reactor (accessed 15 February 2024).

25. Lawrence Livermore National Laboratory. (n.d.). LLNL's national ignition facility delivers record laser energy. Press release. https://www.llnl.gov/article/50616/llnls-national-ignition-facility-delivers-record-laser-energy (accessed 1 February 2024).

26. US Department of Energy. (2023). DOE announces $42 million for inertial fusion energy hubs. Press release (7 December). https://www.energy.gov/articles/doe-announces-42-million-inertial-fusion-energy-hubs (accessed 20 December 2023).

27. Chugh, A., and Taibi, E. (2021). What is green hydrogen and why do we need it? An expert explains. World Economic Forum (21 December). https://www.weforum.org/agenda/2021/12/what-is-green-hydrogen-expert-explains-benefits (accessed 20 December 2023).

28. US Office of Energy Efficiency and Renewable Energy. (n.d.). Hydrogen fuel basics. https://www.energy.gov/eere/fuelcells/hydrogen-fuel-basics (accessed 12 December 2023).

29. Duke Energy. (2023). Duke Energy announces plans to build and operate the nation's first system capable of producing, storing and combusting 100% green hydrogen in a combustion turbine in Florida. *CSR Wire*. Press release (8 November). https://www.csrwire.com/press_releases/787986-duke-energy-announces-plans-build-and-operate-nations-first-system-capable (accessed 20 December 2023).

30. Bloom Energy. (n.d.). The world's largest and most efficient solid oxide electrolyzer. Press release. https://www.bloomenergy.com/bloomelectrolyzer/?utm_device=c&utm_matchtype=p&utm_term=electrolyzer&utm_campaign=7A-Hydrogen-Electrolyzer&utm_source=Google&utm_medium=CPC&hsa_acc=9429233231&hsa_cam=19877486618&hsa_

grp=152064326634&hsa_ad=658353020398&hsa_src=g&hsa_tgt=kwd-3389740665004&hsa_kw=electrolyzer&hsa_mt=p&hsa_net=adwords&hsa_ver=3&gad_source=1&gclid=Cj0KCQiA7OqrBhD9AR IsAK3UXh01mhkKFG4_ZVk1Gy6NrvwwWvg6En_YIc4t3edpI· LEU1CkzMIojRxIaAhmREALw_wcB (accessed 20 December 2023).

31. SoCalGas Newsroom. (2023). SoCalGas issues statement on Gov. Gavin Newsom's strategy to develop a hydrogen economy of the future in California. Press release (9 August). https://newsroom.socalgas.com/press-release/socalgas-issues-statement-on-gov-gavin-newsoms-strategy-to-develop-a-hydrogen-economy (accessed 20 December 2023).

32. ZeroAvia. (2023). ZeroAvia engines to power ecojet. Press release (28 November) https://zeroavia.com/ecojet (accessed 2 December 2023).

33. Airbus. (n.d.). ZEROe towards the world's first hydrogen-powered commercial aircraft. https://www.airbus.com/en/innovation/low-carbon-aviation/hydrogen/zeroe (accessed 20 December 2023).

34. H2Fly. (2023). H2Fly and partners complete world's first piloted flight of liquid hydrogen-powered electric aircraft. Press release (7 September). https://www.h2fly.de/2023/09/07/h2fly-and-partners-complete-worlds-first-piloted-flight-of-liquid-hydrogen-powered-electric-aircraft (accessed 20 November 2023).

35. US Energy Information Administration. (n.d.). Hoover Dam hydroelectric plant. https://www.eia.gov/kids/for-teachers/field-trips/hoover-dam-hydroelectric-plant.php#:~:text=At%20the%20Hoover%20Dam%2C%20there,produce%202%2C080%20megawatts%20of%20power (accessed 10 December 2023).

36. Water Science School. (2018). Three Gorges dam world's largest hydroelectric plant. USGS (6 June). https://www.usgs.gov/special-topics/water-science-school/science/three-gorges-dam-worlds-largest-hydroelectric-plant#:~:text=Use%20topics%20%E2%80%A2Three%20Gorges%20Dam%3A%20The%20world's%20largest%20hydroelectric%20plant,the%20world's%20largest%20hydroelectric%20facility (accessed 10 November 2023).

37. Ibid.

38. We Build Value. (2022). Lake Mead: Drought empties lake and puts third intake into action. *We Build Value Digital Magazine* (18 May). https://www.webuildvalue.com/en/stories-behind-projects/lake-mead-new-intake.html (accessed 10 December 2023).

39. US Office of Energy Efficiency and Renewable Energy. (n.d.). What is pumped storage hydropower? https://www.energy.gov/eere/water/pumped-storage-hydropower (accessed 10 December).

40. Uria-Martinez, R., and Johnson, M. (2023). U.S. hydropower market report 2023. US Department of Energy. https://www.energy.gov/sites/default/files/2023-09/U.S.%20Hydropower%20Market%20Report%202023%20Edition.pdf (accessed 10 December 2023).
41. Maloney, P. (2018). Los Angeles considers $3B pumped-storage project at Hoover Dam. UtilityDive (26 July). https://www.utilitydive.com/news/los-angeles-considers-3b-pumped-storage-project-at-hoover-dam/528699 (accessed 10 December 2023).
42. Kilcher, L., Fogarty, M., and Lawson, M. (2021). Marine energy in the United States: An overview of opportunities. National Renewable Energy Laboratory (February). https://www.nrel.gov/docs/fy21osti/78773.pdf (accessed 10 December 2023).
43. Cart, J. (2023). Blue power: Will ocean waves be California's new source of clean energy? CalMatters (29 November). https://calmatters.org/environment/2023/11/ocean-energy-waves-california (accessed 2 December 2023).
44. McDermott-Murphy, C., and McMurtry, T. (2023). Designing the future of wave energy. National Renewable Energy Laboratory. Press release (21 March). https://www.nrel.gov/news/program/2023/designing-the-future-of-wave-energy.html (accessed 10 December 2023).
45. Kilcher et al., Marine energy in the United States.

Chapter 11

1. Info.gov. (n.d.). Sarbanes-Oxley Act of 2002. https://www.govinfo.gov/content/pkg/COMPS-1883/pdf/COMPS-1883.pdf (accessed 30 November 2023).
2. ClimateWatch. (n.d.). Historical GHG emissions. https://www.climatewatchdata.org/ghg-emissions?source=Climate%20Watch (accessed 2 December 2023).
3. United Nations Climate Action. (n.d.). Food and climate change: Healthy diets for a healthier planet. https://www.un.org/en/climatechange/science/climate-issues/food (accessed 4 December 2023).
4. Waite, R., and Zoints, J. (2022). 7 opportunities to reduce emissions from beef production. World Resources Institute (7 March 20). https://www.wri.org/insights/opportunities-reduce-emissions-beef-production (accessed 3 December 2023).
5. CLEAR Center. (2020). Why methane from cattle warms the climate differently than CO2 from fossil fuels. UC Davis (7 July). https://clear.ucdavis.edu/explainers/why-methane-cattle-warms-climate-differently-co2-fossil-fuels (accessed 22 January 2024).

6. Quinton, A. (2019). Cows and climate change: Making cattle more sustainable. UC Davis (27 June). https://www.ucdavis.edu/food/news/making-cattle-more-sustainable (accessed 3 December 2023).

7. Ibid.

8. Shurtleff, W., and Aoyagi, A. (2004). History of tofu. Soy Info Center. https://www.soyinfocenter.com/HSS/tofu1.php (accessed 29 January 2024).

9. Connolly, M. (2013). Timeline: A short and sweet history of fake meat. *Mother Jones* (November–December). https://www.motherjones.com/environment/2013/12/history-fake-meat (accessed 2 January 2024).

10. Imarc. (2024). Plant-based meat market report by product type. https://www.imarcgroup.com/plant-based-meat-market#:~:text=Market%20Overview%3A,22.4%25%20during%202024%2D2032 (accessed 29 January 2024).

11. Post, M. (2013). Launch of world's first cultured meat hamburger. YouTube video (5 August). https://www.youtube.com/watch?v=slslQLZL2EI (accessed 4 December 2023).

12. US EIA. (2024). Hawaii state energy profile (18 January). https://www.eia.gov/state/print.php?sid=HI#:~:text=Hawaii%20Quick%20Facts&text=In%202022%2C%20about%2029%25%20of,total%20generation%20came%20from%20renewables (accessed 29 January 2024).

13. Tesla. (n.d.). Megapack: Massive energy storage. https://www.tesla.com/megapack (accessed 29 January 2024).

14. Lambert, F. (2024). Tesla megapack battery turns on to replace Hawaii's last coal plant. Electrek (11 January). https://electrek.co/2024/01/11/tesla-megapack-battery-turns-on-replace-hawaii-last-coal-plant (accessed 29 January 2024).

15. Walmart. (n.d.). Sustainability. https://corporate.walmart.com/purpose/sustainability (accessed 3 December 2023).

Addendum I

1. Independent Petroleum Association of America. (n.d.). Hydraulic fracturing. https://www.ipaa.org/fracking; Office of Fossil Energy and Carbon Management (n.d.). Hydraulic fracturing technology. US Department of Energy. https://www.energy.gov/fecm/hydraulic-fracturing-technology (accessed 7 December 2023).

Index